HAUNTED TAVERNS

DONALD STUART

TEMPUS

First published 2007

Tempus Publishing Limited
Cirencester Road, Chalford
Stroud, Gloucestershire, GL6 8PE
www.tempus-publishing.com

British Library Cataloguing in Publication Data.
A catalogue record for this book is available from the British Library.

ISBN 978 0 7524 4347 8

Typesetting and origination by Tempus Publishing Limited.
Printed in Great Britain.

HAUNTED
TAVERNS

CONTENTS

INTRODUCTION

Many people who adamantly maintain they have no belief in ghosts and apparitions are still open to religious beliefs and magazine horoscopes. Which, when considered, imply that they have some belief in matters outside their immediate knowledge.

Stories about ghosts have been around for over 2,000 years and in old cultures such as American Indians and Australian Aborigines, they have always been visited by long-dead relations, and accept them as being part of their present-day world.

In this country the Celt is particularly open to this manner of thinking; a banshee, for example, is the ghost of a dead person that can only be seen by a close relative. Many years ago, the Celts and other Gaelic peoples would throw the most valuable possession of a dead person into a river or loch for them carry into the afterlife.

For those who do believe in ghosts and haunting it is often maintained that these are souls who have not completed something on earth; it could be revenge or hatred or immense sorrow at being cut off from life too early. Some believe that they did not have the entrance fee to the other world. Religion has it that unless we behave well on earth we cannot get into heaven; is that not paying something? This was firmly believed in Roman and Greek mythology where dead people crossed the river Styx, (the river of hate), ferried by Charon, the old ferry man. Charon would only take dead souls who had been buried with a coin on their mouths for him, an ancient Greek silver coin, the obol. Sailors have always worn a gold earring to pay for their funeral if they wash up dead from the sea.

As late as the early nineteenth century cats were walled up into new buildings to prevent attack by the devil or other evil beings. Witchmarks were common and I have come across them at two pubs: the Fleece at Brentforten and the Royalist Hotel at Stow-on-the-Wold. These marks, between 3-500 years old and usually near the fireplace or the hearth, kept the witches at bay.

One of the oldest ghost stories was recorded by Pliny the Younger in the first century BC. Pliny described a house at Athens where, during the night, there was a clanking of chains and, 'the hideous phantom of an old man who seemed the very picture of abject filth and misery,' and went on to describe him having fetters around his legs and shackles of links of iron around his wrists. Anyone viewing this apparition was described as being driven out of their senses. However a philosopher, Athendorus, came across the house that was to let. He moved in and when the ghost appeared he pointed out that he was too busy to deal with him at the time. The ghost beckoned him out into the garden. Athendorus put down his parchment and followed. He found a grave and when this was dug up, there was the skeleton of a murdered man bound in chains. After this skeleton had been properly buried, and the house cleansed by ritual, the old philosopher went back to his thinking and writing, completely undisturbed.

In my lifetime I have had two very curious happenings that I have never been able to explain. On one occasion I was cycling along a lane near Holywell, Cambridgeshire, when I saw a woman cycling towards me. She was on an old sit-up-and-beg bicycle with a basket on the front, and her dark hair piled up over her head in the style of the 1940s. She wore a dark blue or mauve frock with large, red spots on it. At that moment I was distracted by a cuckoo in a nearby field and looked across to a wood. When I turned around the woman and cycle had disappeared. The offside of the road to me was hedged by huge fur trees and fencing and there was no house or lane she could have taken to get off the road. On the second occasion, a bow tie that I kept on a shelf in my kitchen, disappeared. When I went out to my back garden for the first time on that day, the tie was lying on a path and, although it had been raining all night, was dry to the touch.

As far as ghosts haunting pubs is concerned, it may well be that they are so very old and where many strange things have taken place.

There was a coarse joke told in my childhood in Yorkshire – 'Our family was so poor they could not afford senna pods. They sat the kids on a pot and told them ghost stories'.

A-Z

Bedfordshire

Cross Keys, Pulloxhill

By night this pub, 500-years-old, is home to a Cavalier officer murdered nearby. He has been seen in a plumed hat with a neatly pointed beard and long cloak. Now, because of the number of ghostly sightings at this inn, it has been raised to a Grade 5 on the Haunted List. Grade 6 is where an actual photograph is produced. It has been checked by the Phantom Society and other investigators, who saw several people and blue lights moving across the bar-room floor. A woman, dressed in grey, has been seen sitting in the inglenook fireplace, as has a man in a brown, 1930s suit, recognised by a regular as a former landlord. Several customers will not sit near the fire as they say it makes the hair on their neck rise. In one case a stranger was having a meal near the fireplace when a cast-iron lion, from above the fireplace, fell onto his plate although it had been securely fixed. This lion can be seen on the shelf on the right-hand side of the picture.

Berkshire

Bull, Wargrave

A large corner inn, the Bull was built in the fifteenth century as a coaching inn and has many ancient features including part of the old stone wall from an earlier building. Sounds of a weeping woman can be heard from one room here. A previous landlord discovered his wife was having an affair and kicked her out of house and home. He refused to let her see her only child ever again. Every now and again she can be heard in the pub, keening and mourning this dreadful incident. There is also the ghost of a tall man wearing a black hat who makes an appearance from time to time. He is usually seen sitting near the huge open log fire.

George Hotel, Wallingford

Taken into madness after her lover was killed, a young woman living here spent all her time in one room. She used her time mixing her salt tears with soot and painting the wall with marks.

Left: *Cross Keys, Pulloxhill*

Below: *Bull, Wargrave*

This room is known as the Tear Drop Room. The phantom of this former landlord's daughter has been seen by several people. It is usually in the middle of the night when she is seen and she is weeping, with a tear- ravaged face. As soon as she is spoken to she glides back into the wall of the Tear Drop Room. There is also the earthly spirit of a man who was hanged on newly erected gallows nearby in 1626. It was opened in 1517 as an inn and then known as the George & Dragon.

Leathern Bottle, Warfield

Over 150 years ago a dreadful murder took place at this inn. Hannah Carey, the wife of the landlord had been caught having an affair with a local man and her husband found out. He started beating her up, and, on one occasion, jumped up and down on her in a jealous, black rage. She was seriously injured and died a month later from her injuries and he was duly hanged for murder. Now the pair is still in residence with loud and dreadful oaths from him and weeping sounds from the unfortunate Hannah.

Seven Stars, Knowl Hill

Originally this was a religious symbol and also the sign of the Worshipful Company of Innkeepers. At least four phantoms still roam the pub and the immediate area; a horseman dressed overall in black, a woman who parades minus her head and a phantom dog with a woman dressed in white wearing an old- fashioned bonnet. This is one of the oldest inns in Berkshire and was once home to highwaymen and other criminal elements.

Buckinghamshire

Chequers Inn, Amersham

Often where religious martyrs have been executed there are reports of ghostly happenings. At this fifteenth-century inn there are documented details of a hooded figure in a long white gown or dress, in a bedroom. She is thought to be the spirit of a woman who was obliged to start the fire that executed her father. This has been accompanied by loud wailing and cries. Another indwell is said to be that of a Mr Osman who was warden to seven martyrs burned at the stake; he is still with us in spirit as some atonement. A large monument to the seven stands on a hill a few hundred yards from the inn.

George & Dragon, West Wycombe

The little indwell here is a young girl who was a servant at the pub many years ago. Susan, or Sukie, as she was known, fell in love with a highwayman and the local youths were angry about this because she preferred someone like that to one of them. She was tricked into going to some nearby caves by a bogus letter where the youths taunted her and threw stones. Susan was seriously injured by one of these stones and taken back to this inn where she died. She still haunts the stairwell and landing of this fifteenth-century coaching inn dressed all in white. Some male guests have reported being stroked by icy fingers as they slept and one landlord saw a woman on the stairs who suddenly disappeared. There have also been footsteps heard at the inn and are said to be a man, a traveller, who was robbed and murdered here in the eighteenth century and he is wandering about looking for his assailants and valuables. The children of a former landlady used to talk of a 'nice' lady in white coming out of a cupboard and talking to them. The boy said that she seemed to be wearing a pink headband which could well have been a blood-stained bandage.

Seven Stars, Knowl Hill

Little Angel Inn, Remenham

An old story at this pub is of a woman, Mary Blandy, who murdered her father on the premises and is still in residence. Mary Blandy is also said to haunt the nearby lanes on a phantom white horse. She was in love with a married man and her father disapproved. After her trial she was hanged at Oxford in 1752 and a play all about her has been produced at the Kenton Theatre, Henley on Thames on several occasions. Curious things have happened there, too. Once, when some members of the cast were discussing her, a cup leaped from a table a good 6ins-high and smashed onto the ground. At the pub apparitions and chills have marked her returning to the scene of the crime.

Chequers Inn, Amersham

Little Angel Inn, Remenham

Ostrich, Colnbrook

The original building was a hospice run by monks going back 800 years. It is thought that the word hospice was corrupted to its present name, Ostrich. A terrible story of murder lies behind this attractive inn. A former licensee murdered at least sixty people at the hotel in the seventeenth century. This landlord, Jarman, put some of his wealthier guests into a special room. He built a trap of a hinged bed that pitched them into vats of ale. Some of the guests have not left the premises and can be heard weeping and crying out through the night. The landlord was hanged for his grisly crimes. One victim, a wealthy merchant named Coln, was found dead in the local stream and is said to give rise to the original name of Coln-in-the-Brook. King John is reputed to have stayed here on his way to sign the *Magna Carta Liberatum* at Runneymede in 1215.

Royal Standard of England, Beaconsfield

It started as an alehouse in Saxon times when it was known as *Se Scip*, the Ship, and is the oldest free house in England. It was patronised by royalty when they were hunting in the area and also by monks and pilgrims moving between the abbeys and monasteries. By the fourteenth century it found much of its business from salt merchants and cattle drovers. The roads were dangerous, because of robbers, and a decree was passed in 1304 cutting the brushwood back to 200yds each side of the track to prevent ambush. By the end of the seventeenth century the inn was offering separate rooms instead of the usual communal area. During the English Civil War some twelve Cavaliers were executed outside the pub; one a drummer boy aged twelve whose ghost still haunts the inn. Because the inn had given much support to the Royalist cause, Charles II said that from then on it would be called the Royal Standard of England. It has been well known as a haunted inn with the drummer boy, an invisible hand that tugs and pulls at sleeves during mealtimes, a shadowy woman who moves about in the ladies' lavatory, one man who strides across a bar and through a wall and the ghost of a traveller who was killed by a speeding coach outside the pub driven by a mad young rake from the Four Horse Club.

Watts Arms, Hanslope

A somewhat fearsome apparition took up abode here in June 1830. He was 'Highland Hercules', Alex McKay, who was a well known bare-knuckle fighter of the time. He died after a fight lasting forty-seven rounds with 'Emerald Gem' Burns nearby. He was carried back to the pub but never regained consciousness. Although it was known the pub was haunted for many years it was not until a writer on fist fighting went to the pub and recognised McKay for whom he was and was able to supply dates. The pub is named after a local landowning family, one of whom was murdered by his gamekeeper in 1912.

Cambridgeshire

Black Bull, Brampton and the Dragon, Brampton

A drummer boy was murdered between these two pubs by a sailor in 1780. The boy's ghost appeared to Gervase Matchem, the murderer, on Salisbury Plain after he made his escape and obliged him to confess, which he did. Matchem was hanged at Huntingdon and gibbeted at Brampton. For years his skeleton swung in the village. Some of the village boys played a prank on another and suggested he offer some hot broth to the corpse to revive him. The boy climbed up a ladder to the skull of Matchem with the soup and, as he offered it another boy, with a very deep voice said, 'Cool it'. The lad fell off, crashed his head, and remained an idiot to the end of

Golden Lion Hotel, St Ives

his days. Matchem is still seen walking about in the village between the two pubs wearing old-fashioned, seafaring garb and occasionally appearing in the bars of each pub.

Golden Lion Hotel, St Ives

The indwell, who makes an appearance here, is a woman in green. Doors open by themselves and, in one case, a guest had the bedclothes ripped from her. There have also been reports of pictures crashing off walls and bells ringing during the night without being set off by human hand. Legend has it that this inn is haunted by Oliver Cromwell. On the thirteenth day of each month Cromwell's ghost walks along a balcony to a room in which he once stayed. One man had all the clothes whipped off his bed and had a struggle to get them back on again. The Cambridge University Society for Psychical Research was called in some thirty years ago but nothing happened during their visit. But, it seemed that 'they' knew, and as soon as the experts had left they were up to their antics again. Bells would ring all over the place, beer taps would run and doors burst open of their own accord. The Green Lady and a Cavalier have been seen to glide across rooms and then disappear through walls. A strange ghost boat has been to be seen sailing up the river from the Wash and moor up behind this pub.

Old Ferry Boat, Holywell

Old Ferry Boat, Holywell

Every year on 17 March a vigil is kept in the pub for the ghost of Juliet Tousley, a young girl whose spirit still roams this riverside inn. She is said to have died from a broken heart after a love affair with Tom Zoul went wrong. This riverside inn has been on the site for over 1,000 years and is one of the oldest in the country. It was, at one time, a monastic ferry house for local monks. Now once a year a special licence is granted for the watch for Juliet. She has been seen to enter the pub and point to a flagstone where it is thought she was buried. There is some evidence that this pub has been here since AD 560 although the first documents available are dated 1100. There is, of course, a holy well, where lepers and others afflicted, came to drink the miracle waters in the Middle Ages. The inn had connections with Hereward the Wake who raised an army to fight William the Conqueror in 1070.

Cheshire

Blue Bell Inn, Tushingham

A fourteenth-century black-and-white-timbered building, the Blue Bell has a ghost duck and other apparitions. Try telling your friends you were enjoying a decent pint of beer when suddenly a duck waddled past and no one else saw it. The story is that many years ago a former landlord killed a duck and buried it in a wall but it has kept returning. At one time a priest exorcised the pub but the ghost duck has taken no notice of this. The landlady tells of poltergeist activities where drawers are opened and closed in her daughter's room.

Orange Tree, Altrincham

This was a common name for pubs after the fruit had been brought to this country by Sir Thomas Gresham in the sixteenth century. The tale of the man who sold his wife in the novel *The Mayor of Casterbridge* actually happened at this pub in 1823. He sold his wife to another man for 1s 6d to get some more beer. In some towns a husband could legally sell his wife on the market place. At one such market a chimney sweep called Cupid Hodson sold his wife for less than 30p. There are four recorded different ghosts here. One woman spoke to a man in the bar who then disappeared into the fireplace and another man in Victorian clothing has been seen in the cellar. Two others, a man and a woman, have been seen and heard chatting in a bar.

Royal George, Knutsford

Gentleman Edward Higgins was a minor aristocrat who doubled as a housebreaker and robber by night. This hostelry, dating from the fourteenth century, was his favourite watering hole until he was taken away and hanged in 1767. He is still with us at the hotel, arrayed in all his period finery. After his arrest he was held in the barred cellar and used some rough chalk to draw a picture of himself on the wall. Although this has been scrubbed off with bleach or covered with paint it still reappears. Phantom coaches have also been seen and heard arriving and departing and dropping passengers. Mrs Elizabeth Gaskell based her novel *Cranford* on the town. She has been said to still haunt the round room here where she did much of her work.

Cornwall

Bucket of Blood, Phillack

Originally called the New Inn, this pub was renamed on the back of a gory legend. Many years ago a landlord went to his well to draw up water. Up came a bucket of blood from a severely mutilated corpse that had been thrown down the well. Now a phantom wearing torn and wet clothing is seen, along with chills. The inn is part twelfth century and is also haunted by a monk in a brown habit and a poltergeist that moves furniture about.

Bush Inn, Morwenstow

This is another pub which claims to be the oldest in the land. It does date back to about AD 940 and originally, a hermit's cave offering food and shelter to pilgrims. It is situated in an isolated area and was, at one time, a resting place for pilgrims on their way between Wales and Spain. Historians have also discovered signs of an even earlier Celtic architecture at the pub. In the graveyard there are buried at least forty unknown men who were washed up from the sea from wrecked ships. Some years ago, at a nearby manor, a haunted chest that was brought back from the Spanish Armada, revealed an evil spirit. Many times the pub has been tested by various groups for ghosts and paranormal events have been reported. The late landlord, Jim Gregory, had a problem with one door that was found open every morning. Several times he wired it up with stronger material each time but every morning the wire was lying on the ground. People staying here have reported an elderly, seafaring man sitting on a four-poster bed and people on the staircase who disappeared when spoken to.

Interior of the Bush Inn, Morwenstow

Exterior of the Bush Inn, Morwentstow

Crumplehorn Inn, Polperro

An ancient inn that appears in the *Domesday Book* is haunted by an elderly man and, sometimes, a young woman. There is also the legend of Willy Willcock's Hole. He was a fisherman at Polperro and a customer at this pub who, when exploring the caves nearby, got lost and he is still in there. He can be heard crying as he wanders the maze of passages trying to find an exit. Almost three centuries ago there was a most cunning local parson, Richard Dodge. He claimed to be a ghost hunter and exorcist which was a cover for his secondary job as a smuggler. He told people that the Devil himself haunted certain parts of the beach and this kept honest people away at nights.

Jamaica Inn, Bolventor

Probably one of the best known inns in the world, over 200 years old, this was immortalised by Daphne du Maurier. She lived nearby in the 1930s. Here an old sailor in long sea coat and tricorne hat has been seen sitting on a wall of the inn and then disappearing into the road. He is thought to be a sailor who was murdered here many years ago. The inn was built in 1789 as a posting station. About 1 ½miles to the south is Dozmary Pool where King Arthur is said to have thrown the sword Excalibur before he died. A photograph taken recently by a man and his daughter in one room at the inn showed a man with a shaven head, as a convict would have appeared, and dressed in ragged clothing.

Jolly Sailor Inn, Looe

When two licensees moved in recently one of the first things they came across was the pub ghost. He was wearing a frock-coated uniform of a coachman or stable boy with a ruffed shirt, hair in a pony tail and leather gaiters. He has been seen on many occasions over the years and a porter, (an ex-police officer), reported sighting of a young girl passing through walls on the landing. A small woman, dressed in old-fashioned clothing, has been viewed as she moved between bedrooms and she has even spoken to guests or employees.

Miner's Arms, Mithian

One of the most fascinating inns in Cornwall, it was built in 1557 and has a large number of small rooms on different levels and a stone-flagged floor. There is an Elizabethan frieze on the ceiling of one room, wood-blocked floors and a wall painting of Queen Elizabeth I. The penance cupboard, on the stairs, is where people on the run from religious persecution hid before escaping down into a cellar and through a secret passage to a nearby manor house. One photograph in the pub, taken in late-Victorian times, shows a group of people at the manor house and includes two children in sailor suits with their backs to the camera, but who should not be there. This was by comparison with other prints from the same negative. Other ghosts have been seen walking along the passageway past the bar towards the penance cupboard in old-fashioned clothing.

Napoleon Inn, Boscastle

Built in 1549 the Napoleon has a splendid ghost nicknamed Plucker. He is often seen standing near the fireplace and guests and drinkers there have had their arms tugged and pulled. Plucker seems particularly active when there has been some redecoration in the pub. On one occasion he managed to take a pile of coins out of the safe and stacked them up next to plastic bags on the bar top. One landlady was locked into a utility room as a key turned on her although no one was there. A recently hung picture jumped off a wall as an elderly woman was watching television, and a radiator, well fixed, fell off a wall.

Jamaica Inn, Bolventor

Miner's Arms, Mithian

Punch Bowl Inn, Lanreath

Now here is a rum story to be sure. This inn is said to be haunted by an old black cockerel that is the earthbound spirit of a former rector of the village. He met with an accident when he fell down the cellar steps at his nearby vicarage on his way to get some more wine for dinner. His guest that night was the new curate, who had fallen in love with the parson's daughter, and had sought her hand in marriage. Rumour has it that there had been a violent row between the two men before the parson's demise. The next day the black cockerel flew in through the open window of the pub and has been in residence ever since. As it flew in on one occasion it finished up in an earthenware pot and a scullery maid put the lid on to keep him in. After this a mason was called to seal the poor bird in for ever but, now and again, he makes his spirit voice heard.

Wellington Hotel, Boscastle

One of the historic coaching inns of Cornwall and one man who called here never left. On several occasions a man has been seen wearing an eighteenth-century coachman's uniform of frock coat, frilled shirt, gaiters and heavy boots. Under his hat his hair is tied back as it would have been at that time. Another apparition has been seen and said to be that of a young girl who took her own life while unhappy in love. A third spirit has been spotted wandering down into the cellar as a very dark outline. There is another curious ghost that was followed across a room by a dog belonging to a writer of ghost stories who was staying at the inn. Sadly for the writer he never saw the apparition himself.

Cumbria

Dalston Hall, Dalston

An inscription reads 'John Dalston, Elisabet, my wyf mad ys building' in Gothic script on this sixteenth-century building. Above the manorial hall is a gallery and it is here where the oldest ghost in the building is seen. She is wearing Tudor-style dress and known to all as Lady Jane. At the bottom of the stairs is an ancient doorway that leads to a staircase and a heavy iron gate. The staircase spirals up with worn stone steps and comes out at the honeymoon suite. One cupboard was opened and there was found another staircase that goes to a blank wall with strange sounds coming from behind it. There have been sounds from the cellars as though wooden beer barrels were being rolled about. One man went down to investigate and saw a man working but was told by reception that no one was in there at all. Room four is said to be haunted by the ghost of a maid servant who worked there many years ago and who died when she threw herself from the pele tower above that room. Room twelve, a honeymoon suite, has a four-poster bed and people who have stayed there have been awakened by girls' voices whispering and giggling and a feeling they are being watched. There is a Victorian handyman ghost seen working in the grounds who disappears when spoken to.

Edenhall Hotel, near Penrith

There are several ghosts here where the building dates from the early 1600s and include at least two women and a man. One owner slept in an attic room with a ceiling that slopes down on each side with a skylight and curious trapdoors. He reported seeing an elderly woman in Victorian or Edwardian dress. One woman who worked at the hotel for twenty years, was on her way up to an attic bedroom. She saw a woman walking in front of her and thought it was another maid called Irene but who then disappeared. Bar staff have noticed a man walk past in a mirror behind guests and then disappear. A waitress tells of an old woman sitting in an armchair in a corner, but, when she looked back, the woman had disappeared. In one guest room there is a sunken bath with a mirror behind it and a number of guests have said that a woman walked out of the mirror while they were in the bath and sometimes she would appear at the end of their bed.

Gosforth Hall Hotel, Gosforth

Gosforth Hall was built by Robert Copley in 1658 and he built a priest's hole into the chimney stack, for those were parlous times. People have been awakened by whispered conversations in their room and poltergeists have run amok in the kitchen. Faces have also been seen peering through upper windows. The main ghost is a monk who is seen walking along corridors and disappearing into rooms and one member of staff has a presence – breathing down the back of the neck every time she goes to the lavatory. Room eleven has a large four-poster bed and it is in this room that many people have seen an apparition sitting near the priest's hole. Also in room eleven it is said that the original family had a retarded child and it was chained up in here. Recently there have been sounds of an iron chain dragging across a floor with a child weeping.

Kirkstone Pass Inn, Ambleside

The highest pub in Cumbria, it stands at the top of the pass and a sign outside the inn says it was built in 1496. There have been many reports over the years of people seeing ghosts and apparitions about the place and, on one occasion, a woman went out and slept in her car because she was so fearful. One family staying there just before Christmas told a story of a man standing at the bar in mid-1700s costume and assumed he was in fancy dress. A photograph was taken by the man of his wife outside the pub with their son and when it was printed showed a man in a tricorne hat. At the time she felt a pressure on her shoulder and later found a red mark although no one had been near her. A local youth, working there, turned around to see a woman dressed in grey without a face and reaching out to him. There is a copy at the inn of a picture of the Revd Sewell, who rebuilt the inn, and a man appears behind him, but this figure does not appear in the original painting. Outside there is an old tree called the hangman's tree and a female ghost is seen here and said to have been hanged from it for murdering her child. A woman who works at the pub said recently:

> I was having a cup of tea late one afternoon when a customer said to me that there were some ghosts standing behind me. Of course I turned round and I saw nothing. The lady then got up and stood behind me talking to those ghosts. She later explained that the ghosts were unsettled because they had been executed on the hanging tree that was originally where I was sat. They told her that they had not deserved to be executed for their petty crimes. The lady was from Keswick and she said that she comes to the pub every few months and always sees some ghosts.

On several occasions pictures have come off walls and been found neatly arranged some distance away.

Moresby Hall, Moresby

The building dates back to 1690 and the façade is ornate. When the hall was being renovated many years ago an old-stone floor was taken up and underneath were eight skeletons. The police investigated and passed the case on to the local archaeological association which reported they were Roman bodies and had probably come from a burial ground near the old fort. When the

Kirkstone Pass Inn, Ambleside

building was being renovated in 1998 the skeleton of a small child was found inside the huge chimney breast. In 1715 one of the Fletchers, who owned the hall, was taken to London and questioned about his Jacobite sympathies and tried for treason. He forgot to tell servants that another Jacobite was in hiding in a secret room, who then starved to death. It is this unfortunate man and the small child who haunt the hotel.

Overwater Hotel, Ireby

Joseph Gillbanks, born 1780, set himself up as a merchant trading from Jamaica, made a fortune, and married the niece of the chief justice there. Then he began an affair with a poor black girl on the island. In 1814 he returned from the West Indies with his wife and bought Overwater Hall. Prosperous and genteel he became a local magistrate and had the motto, *Honore and Virtute*, carved over the entrance. Then the black girl from Jamaica found him and claimed she was pregnant. First of all he took her out in a boat and tried to drown her and when she tried to get back in the boat he took a sword to her and chopped off her arms. He was never pursued for her murder although some of the facts had come out and he died aged seventy-three in his bed. She, however, is still with us. Since then it has become an hotel and guests and staff report seeing the ghost of a black girl with no arms and a headdress or large bonnet who usually appears at New Year and there is a tapping on the window outside. Legend has it that Overwater Tarn never freezes over because, even in the coldest winter, a severed black hand and arm pushes through and breaks up the ice. Another apparition about the place is a grey terrier dog seen inside the hotel.

Derbyshire

Bell Hotel, Derby

At the Bell Hotel the Tudor fronting was added after the First World War to an inn built in 1680. There are several ghosts here. The first is the Victorian Lady who suddenly appears in a bar and then slowly disappears in front of people. A poltergeist exists and on one occasion threw a wooden coat hanger that struck a barmaid on the back of the head. A servant girl has been seen on many occasions dressed in eighteenth-century fashion in an upstairs room. Rumour has it that she had been killed by Scottish rebels in 1745. Sometimes she is seen when children have been taken ill and she is seen bending over them and patting them on the back to make them better.

Castle Inn, Castleton

A very sensible jollification takes place every year on 29 May when a Garland Day is held to celebrate the restoration of Charles II. High above the village lays Peveril Castle that forms the basis for Sir Walter Scott's novel, *Peveril of the Peaks*. At this seventeenth-century inn is the earthly spirit of a girl who was ditched at the altar steps and there are still sounds of her crying as her wedding feast is being prepared. Even more horrific old lore has it that a woman was buried in the foundations of the inn and still wanders. There is also a man dressed in a pin-stripe suit with an old English sheepdog. Winnats Pass, a gorge near the town on the old turnpike route, is haunted by the spirits of two young lovers murdered by local miners in 1758.

Miner's Arms, Eyam

A number of phantoms and ghosts have been seen in the Miner's Arms over the years. They include two teenaged girls who perished in a fire at the pub many years ago. They were called Sara and Emma and people staying there have heard voices calling out their names. The area was the burial pits for victims of Eyam's plague between 1665 and 1666. The pub itself was built in 1630. Just outside the village is Mompesson's Well where, during the plague, food and clothing was left. Coins would be put out, after being disinfected with vinegar, for the tradesmen. The illness arrived at the village after some infected clothing was sent from London. It is maintained that some of the pub hosts are victims of that plague.

Norfolk Arms Hotel, Glossop

For many years the Norfolk Arms Hotel was a stopping point for coaches going over to Sheffield. It is well known as a haunted pub and over the years many people have seen a little girl of about ten, with blonde ringlets, running along the bar and then disappear. From time to time an exceedingly tall man wearing a long dark coat, in Victorian fashion, has been seen sitting in the lounge bar. Legend has it that he was a coachman who died in an accident nearby over 150 years ago. There are local stories that bare-knuckle fights once took place at the rear of the inn. Several men who were seriously injured died in the pub, which may account for some of the phantoms.

Devon

Bearslake Inn, Okehampton

Over 600 years old, it is a most attractive pub with a resident indwell. Years ago a small girl, Clare, fell from a spiral staircase and died. Now a child can be heard crying at locking up time and has put the wind up quite a few people staying there. Not far away was one of the most feared bogs in Britain,

Bridge Inn, Topsham

since drained. It was haunted by many who had died there but one of the most famous was Bengie Geare, a former mayor of Okehampton. The apparition of Geare appears riding on a black pony.

Bridge Inn, Topsham
When Queen Elizabeth II visited this eleventh-century pub in March 1998 there was no sign of Naughty Nancy, resident ghost. It was Her Majesty's first official visit to a pub. The Queen took away a bottle of special brew from the Bridge saying her husband might well enjoy it. Topsham was once a thriving port with forty-one pubs and twenty-six brothels and it thought that Naughty Nancy took up refuge at the Bridge Inn during these colourful times. She has been seen flitting between the several bars in Victorian dress with a low neckline. Part of the pub building dates back to 1083 when it was built for artisans and masons working on Exeter Cathedral.

Church House Inn, Torbryan
An old coaching inn this was one of the most important between Exeter and Plymouth and built on a Saxon manor. A number of kings including Henry VIII and his father, Henry VII stayed here. It has been described as the most haunted inn in the county and, among the easier ghosts to spot, are a barmaid, an elderly man and a monk. The landlord says that every year people write to him after staying there to tell of the ghosts they have encountered during their visit. On one occasion a housekeeper saw a ghost walk behind the landlord and into a wall. One woman, writing to the landlord, said that the old man, seen in the bar and bedrooms, is named Emmet. During the Second World War a police sergeant went into the bar and spoke to an army officer. He bought him a drink and said to the barman, 'And one for the man at the fireplace'. But, when they turned round, the man had disappeared.

Devil's Stone Inn, Shebbear

A naughty little girl about seven-years-old still wanders this isolated Devon pub. She is believed to be the daughter of a man who was murdered there many years ago. Often she is seen in the company of a grey-bearded man. She is noted for merry pranks and pulling at peoples' hair. Every year the villagers and bell ringers turn over a boulder weighing half a ton to make sure the devil is not hiding underneath. It was a pagan ritual and gave rise to the fourteenth-century pub's name.

Old Inn, Widecombe-in-the-Moor

A sobbing child is heard from an empty room, a large gentleman is seen walking from room to room and then to disappear and the ghost of Tom Pearce's grey mare haunt this inn. There is an old grave, nearby, where fresh flowers have been laid without explanation every year, but no one ever sees who leaves them. Mary Jay, the person buried there, hanged herself in a barn and was buried in unconsecrated ground. She had been deserted by a local farm hand who had made her pregnant. A man dressed in old-fashioned clothes has been seen bending over the grave and then to disappear. Old Uncle Tom Cobleigh (or Cobley) was a local farmer and well known for his amorous dalliances. There was a large number of Cobleighs but the one of the song died in 1794. Drake's ghost has been seen as he crosses the moor in a black coach pulled by headless horses.

Pack o' Cards, Combe Martin

This eccentric building is one the most unusual and the best known inns in the county. In 1690 George Ley won a large amount of money at cards and built the house with the proceeds. It has four floors to represent the card suites, fifty-two windows, fifty-two stairs and is on 52sq ft of ground-floor space. It is not clear when it became an inn but was certainly there in the early-nineteenth century. There are several resident ghosts here that include a woman in a long white dress and a small man with a very long beard. In the hotel is a 'press gang table' that is 10ft long and 4ft wide, built in the refectory style and more than 12ins deep. When news got out that the press gang was in the area to take anyone into the Royal Navy, they would hide in there.

Prospect Inn, Exeter

Not only is this seventeenth-century inn well haunted but there are ghosts and other off-worlders on the historic quay outside. There have been several incidents of a poltergeist making its noisy presence felt and great crashing noise as beer barrels go over in the yard. An annual ghost appearance, usually only on Christmas Day, is a teenaged girl dressed in Victorian clothing, smiling and holding a rag doll. But, on another occasion, she appeared at midsummer and terrified an electrician who was working in the pub. A woman going into the pub heard the sound of horses' hooves behind her. Then she saw a flat-backed Victorian style cart that drove towards the nearby Customs House and disappear into the wall. A yet more exotic haunting is that of a Viking ship sailing up the River Exe towards this quay with a long-haired warrior standing in the prow, waving an angry fist.

Royal Castle Hotel, Dartmouth

When Mary, the wife of William III, first came to Britain she stayed at this hotel. Why she decided to stay here long after her death is a mystery but she is seen from time to time in period costume and her carriage is heard simultaneously moving around in the courtyard outside. Reports have come down that when the coach arrives a passenger is seen to get out and walks into the hotel. This is always at 2 a.m. Beams from a Spanish galleon were used in building

Ship Inn, Exeter

this tavern in 1587. When the coach is heard to arrive there is a loud clattering sound over the cobbles. This is usually between 12 September and late November. The ghost seen here on many occasions is described as 'a nasty little man rather like a jockey and with an evil face'. He is said to be a man called Darke Chase, who had been an ostler at the inn.

Ship Inn, Exeter

A splendidly timbered pub in the old part of Exeter and haunted by none other than the best-known Elizabethan sea dog of all, Drake. There he has been seen on many occasions over the centuries and, sometimes, with other apparitions in sea-going garb. Legend has it that Drake was a noted toper and was often only permitted to drink here if accompanied by a responsible person. He is said to be a bit difficult at times, even today, and when he appears tweaks the ears of people sitting in the bar. Legends sprang up about him even during his life time. The Spaniards firmly believed he had a mirror in which he could see ship movements in any part of the world.

White Hart Hotel, Exeter

An old coaching inn on a road going out of Exeter, it is haunted by several apparitions. The first is described by several witnesses as being a woman of about twenty dressed in a long black cape. She has been seen walking through the courtyard and then up a set of stairs in front of the inn that was taken out many years ago. In another part of the inn there is a bar called Bottlescrew Bill's. From time to time an impish face is seen peering around the end of the bar peering intently at the customers. It is said to be that of a boy aged about five who suddenly disappears whenever a comment is made about him.

Who'd Have Thought It, Milton Combe

Not a common name for a pub, but came about when it was an ale and beer house. They applied for a spirit licence and actually got it at the Brewster Sessions. The inn sign shows the landlord of the time waving his newly granted spirit licence. There are two other spirits here, more wraithlike and not so cheering. Local legend has it that it is the earthly spirit of one Edward Bere a ghostly cavalier who rings for service and that of a former landlord. The pub is sixteenth-century and was closely associated with Sir Francis Drake (1543-1596) who lived at Buckland Abbey nearby. Ancient lore has it that when Drake is needed just beat his drum and he will awake.

Dorset

Angel, Lyme Regis

A ghost, thought to be an old widow landlady who does not want to leave the premises, is heard and seen moving about and opening bolted doors. Several witnesses have described the ghost here as Queen Victoria but it is, in fact, a former proprietor, Mrs Langton. who was here in 1926. She had always insisted in dressing the way the old queen did as she walked about the hotel in the hope of being thought to be the ghost of the old queen. But, when she died in the 1930s, the hotel did become haunted by Queen Victoria (or Mrs Langton). She had set up her own ghost. Mrs Langton has been seen gliding out of cupboards. One man staying there woke up to find the ghost of Queen Victoria or Mrs Langton bending over him.

Ye Olde George Inn, Christchurch

Here, at this six-centuries-old inn, just outside the New Forest, a Grey Lady walks. Some years ago a priest hole was found during renovation work and inside was a torn, old-fashioned shirt

Ye Olde George Inn, Christcurch

Ye Olde George Inn, Christchurch

with shoes and a heap of bones. These have now been removed to the Red House Museum at Christchurch. Licensees over the years have seen plates slowly turning on tables and one particular Victorian print keeps crashing off the wall. Wine bottles that have been put out on separate tables then finish up gathered together on one table. Christchurch was named on a legend that as a church was being built one important beam could not be fitted. A strange carpenter turned up one day and, when all others were sleeping, completed the task. He disappeared and the artisans said they had been helped by Christ himself. In the old coaching courtyard is a mural on the wall showing where the cells used to be for convicted prisoners waiting for the Emerald Coach that took them to Poole to be deported to Australia.

Durham

George Hotel, Piercebridge

Over 100 years ago two brothers named Jenkins ran the George Hotel. They had a long-case clock (a grandfather clock) in the hall. When one died the old clock started losing time and then finally stopped when the other brother died at 4.46 a.m. This gave rise to the song, *My grandfather's clock*. Since then it has been renovated and keeps perfect time. The inn sign, showing George III, is carved in wood with a mouse running up the side. This is the work of the carver, Thompson of Kilburn, who always 'signed' his work with a small mouse. Over the years there have been stories of people hearing voices coming from an empty bar. Some say it is the Jenkins brothers bickering, while others maintain it was two old farmers arguing over the price of cattle. On several occasions there has been seen a figure standing near the clock wearing old-fashioned gaiters.

George Hotel, Piercebridge

Essex

Bell Hotel, Thorpe-le-Soken

A woman, who was married to two men at the same time, including the local vicar, lived nearby. Now she haunts this pub. It is said that when she died, comparatively young, both husbands were at the graveside unknown to each other. She has been known to move heavy furniture about and has been seen to glide through the pub as a shadow that glows white. A presence has been seen and sensed in a guest bedroom and she is described as rather shadowy and moves across the room to disappear through a door. In another guest room a heavy wardrobe has been moved during the night and it seemed that the spare bed in the room had been slept in although no one else had been there. It is said to be the ghost of Kitty Chanham, the eighteenth-century bigamist, who is buried in a nearby graveyard

St Anne's Castle Inn, Great Leighs

After the Witchcraft Act of 1563 there were a large number of hangings in the area around this pub that dates back to the twelfth century. It has, on one outside wall, a painted inscription claiming to be the oldest pub in the country. During the Second World War an excavation was made of an area known as Scrap Faggot Green, the local name for where witches had lived, and disturbed a number of apparitions that still haunt the village and this inn. In recent years a large number of people have tried to sleep in a particular room with a conspicuous lack of success

Swan Hotel, Brentwood

due to cold draughts, curtains being ripped apart and furniture moved. In several cases the bed clothes have been pulled off the cowering occupants. There are reports of black shapes around the bed. During the Second World War some American troops were deployed to widen the road using bulldozers. They were warned that they were moving the Witches' Stone. After this livestock kept disappearing and church bells rang, although this was forbidden during war time. Later the stone was returned and things settled down for a while.

Sun Hotel, Dedham

Here a weeping woman has been seen in bedrooms and on the main landing. She is Eisa, a girl who had worked here, and was burned at the stake as a witch in the pub grounds. Eisa is seen in upstairs bedrooms and on the main staircase. On one occasion a man told Anglia Television that an apparition had held a door open for him. Eisa was the last to be executed for witchcraft in Essex. The county had the worst reputation for executing witches and almost 400 were hanged between 1566 and 1645, many under the investigations of Matthew Hopkins, witch-finder extraordinaire.

Swan Hotel, Brentwood

A mischievous phantom who hides and moves things about at this five-centuries- old inn has even attracted the attention of the local police. Doors opening and closing, cold chills and domestic animals behaving oddly have all been reported. One visitor was spending a night here when there were sudden gusts of cold wind and the strong smell of old leather in his room.

Left: *Berkeley Arms, Tewkesbury*

Opposite: *Butcher's Arms, Sheepscombe, Painswick*

When he got home two days later he found a Latin coin in his pocket that he had never seen before. At the hotel plates fly off the walls and lights are switched on and off. There have been sounds of chairs being dragged about at night. (Police who investigated maintained it was outside their remit to chase ghosts but agreed odd things were happening).

Gloucestershire

Berkeley Arms, Tewkesbury

A quaint and ancient pub in the centre of this historic town, the Berkeley Arms stands in all its timbered glory. After the Battle of Tewkesbury on 4 May 1471 the Duke of Somerset and some of his senior aides were dragged from sanctuary at Tewkesbury Abbey and executed near this inn. Over the past 500 years there have been reports of men in very old-fashioned clothing seen at the inn and sounds as though swords are being sharpened. Over thirty years ago during renovation on an old wall the top of the building was removed. They found a stairway from which there were sounds of someone walking to and fro. Inside, and behind the wall, they found a small room filled with cobwebs and two history books of England dated to 1820. A more-recent ghost is that of a former landlady, Ruby Jones, well known for her astringent tongue and the speed with which she barred unruly customers. Occasionally, when her name is mentioned in the bar, glasses fly off the shelves and have hit customers and barmaids.

THE BUTCHERS ARMS, SHEEPSCOMBE, GLOUCESTERSHIRE

Butcher's Arms, Sheepscombe, Painswick

Dating back to 1670 this pub was opposite the gallows where local rustlers and other ne'er-do-wells were hanged. In the village they had unusual stocks in that they were made of iron with round holes for the hands to go through. They were known as the 'squire's spectacles'. The inn has two women ghosts, one with a phantom dog. There are ninety-nine yew trees in the parish churchyard and it is maintained that this is all that will grow. When a 100th tree is added another one just dies. The name of the pub comes from the time when King Henry VIII hunted in the forests nearby and the carcasses were cut up at this inn.

Corner Cupboard Inn, Winchcombe

This pub looks as though it was made for haunting and was once part of a local monastery. A child is heard running about during the day and there is also lore on phantom monks gliding around the inn. Winchcombe Abbey was destroyed by Henry VIII in 1539. Later excavations at the abbey revealed two stone coffins thought to contain two Saxon kings. A tall, hooded character travels along the road through the village past this pub and towards the graveyard. He is reported as gliding along and about 2ft above the ground.

King's Arms Hotel, Stow-on-the-Wold

Sometimes it is as well not to ask a licensee about any ghost or apparition they have about the place because they are somewhat loath to tell. This was the case at this inn where, instead, a local drinker told of the story behind the phantoms here. He said that a man staying here had gone

Royalist Hotel, Stow-on-the-Wold

into the lounge and saw an elderly woman and a small boy watching television but no one like them were staying at the hotel at the time. Shortly afterwards the two disappeared but reports were that they had been seen by employees and have been seen many times since. Over the years there have been claims it is haunted by Charles I who stayed here in May 1645. Another is an old woman who sits in the lounge alone. Visitors and staff, who have seen her, describe her as being dressed in black with grey hair piled up on top of her head. She wears a chain with a pendant brooch.

Royalist Hotel, Stow-on-the-Wold
A truly ancient inn dating from AD 947, it has a Jacobean facade on the original oak structure and there has been carbon dating that shows the timber to be over 1,000 years old. It was known as the Eagle and Child in the thirteenth-century and originally built by a Saxon duke, Aethelmar and was later used by the Knights of St John's Hospitallers. During restoration work at this inn over the years there has been found a Saxon shoe, a Royalist commander's letters and a tunnel leading to the church. A dowser reported that there was a settlement on the site in AD 514. In the 1970s a curious mark was found – scratch marks into the brickwork of the fireplace and dated as early 1500s. It was the 'witch mark' to keep them away from the house. This inn is well haunted. Firstly by John Shellard, who died in November 1630 aged fifteen, and said to have been done away with by members of his family for property, including the Royalist. A

Ye Olde Black Bear, Tewkesbury

clairvoyant regularly visits the pub and has seen two children in Victorian clothing and there are tapping sounds. Between the bar and reception area visitors have seen a young man smiling at them only to disappear. On the stairs has been seen an elegant woman in a long, lacy dress and a cavalier in full uniform and plumed hat. Two little girl urchins in tattered clothing have been seen weeping outside the inn and a tall knight, arrayed all in black on a landing. Occasionally there have been sounds of music and singing in the middle of the night with no one about.

Tudor House Hotel, Tewkesbury
A black dog still roams this town centre hotel in ancient Tewkesbury. It is also a worthy setting for a White Lady in historic garb. This impressive inn was built in 1540 on the banks of the River Avon. This has been described as the most attractive building in Tewkesbury by the Society for the Preservation of Ancient Buildings. It was built in 1540 and became the local Court of Justice. It is haunted by a woman dressed in a long white gown who is seen on the staircase, but who disappears before reaching any door. The black Labrador dog has been seen standing on the main staircase landing as though guarding it.

Ye Olde Black Bear, Tewkesbury
A truly impressive inn on the corner between town and river. It looks as though it were cunningly contrived for a movie and local legend tells of a headless man dragging chains about the place. The

colour black used as an inn sign was quite common in the eighteenth century. When the Gin Act of 1736 was imposed it meant much higher taxes and many licensees throughout the land draped their inn signs with black velvet or added 'black' to the inn name as a sign of disapproval. The bear is the heraldic feature of many noble families and when associated with the colour black, it refers to the bear baiting that went on until the Oldham Act of 1836 finally made it illegal.

Hampshire

Angel, Lymington

An old coaching inn between Bournemouth and Southampton where a coachman has been seen peering through kitchen windows in the early morning wrapped in voluminous clothes. There is also an old sea dog accoutred in a sea coat with brass buttons. Occasionally there have been sounds of a piano being played in the distance when no one was present. In the pub itself there have been reports of a girl in a long white dress sitting in a chair and thought to be former chambermaid who came to a sad end. A grey-haired man, wearing an old-fashioned naval uniform with brass buttons and fastened at the neck, has been seen on a large number of occasions. This particular apparition is thought to have been an officer awaiting a court enquiry who killed himself in his bedroom. A woman guest heard loud thumping piano music in the middle of the night. The room it came from had been used for years for social occasions but the piano had been taken out and broken up a year previously. There was no other such instrument in the hotel.

Brushmakers Arms, Upham

Once the local headquarters of Oliver Cromwell this former brush factory became a pub in 1644. As a factory, it had been owned by the miser Chickett prior to this, who was murdered in his home for his money. At least two other people came to a violent end here but the miser Chickett can still be heard wandering about and the chink of coins being counted. Clearly there are pockets in a shroud. At one time there was a trade of brush makers locally and they found their materials in the immediate area.

Crown Inn, Alton

It seems a curious feature of hauntings that there are many more human than animal ones. At this inn, the fireplace is a source of great terror to dogs and, when taken near to it, have jumped, barked and fled from the room. Every now and again there can be heard scratching and the whimpers of a dog from the chimney breast even when no such animal is about. There is a story that a drunken farmhand flew into a rage with his dog and beat it to death against the chimney. Then, some years ago, workmen knocking down walls for alterations, removed a false wall near the chimney and found the skeleton of a dog.

Dolphin, Botley

Opened as an inn under the name Dolphin in 1750 it is also reported to have an even earlier history when Cromwell is said to have had headquarters here. There is the history also of the 'Botley Assizes' at the Dolphin. A number of local men held a mock trial on a man for not drinking enough, found him guilty and sentenced him to death. They put a rope around his neck and pulled him up onto the bacon wrack. Legend has it that a party of soldiers came into the square at this point with loud martial music and they all left the pub to watch this and left the hanging man to die. He is said to be still in residence with loud cries. One employee put up a crucifix as an insurance against wandering ghosts in his bedroom.

Dolphin Hotel, High Street, Southampton
Standing below Bar at this ancient port, the Dolphin is built on Norman vaults with a most impressive Georgian frontage. Kings and queens have stayed here; Jane Austen danced with a black-eyed Frenchman at a ball in 1850; and I worked there as a kitchen porter in the 1950s. Tales do abound of Molly, a phantom cleaner, seen in the early hours of the morning drifting along 2ft above the ground. She has also been seen in a main lounge in a grey dress holding a bucket.

Eclipse Inn, Winchester
A woman who supported the Duke of Monmouth in his bid for the throne was executed outside the Eclipse. Lady Alice Lisle sheltered some of his supporters after the Battle of Sedgemoor and was beheaded for it. She spent her last night on earth at this inn. Reports have it of a tall lady walking about the inn wearing a long grey dress and the ghostly sounds of hammering as the execution block is erected. She appealed to the king for clemency after her trial before Judge Jeffreys but this was refused and her body is buried in Ellingham Churchyard. Alice Lisle has also been seen haunting Moyle Court where she had lived and seen in a coach without a driver and two headless horses in Ellingham Lane. At her trial at Winchester Assizes two gentlemen, who disagreed with the verdict, drew their swords to protest, and were later executed themselves.

Above left: *Dolphin, Botley*

Above right: *Eclipse, Winchester*

Above left: *Old Mill Inn, Holbury*

Above right: *Red Lion, Chalton*

Filly Inn, Setley

Set in a picturesque part of the New Forest the Filly features beams, brasses and country implements. It is haunted by the ghost of an old highwayman who preyed on travellers in the seventeenth century. Nearby is the Marlpit Oak where highwaymen gathered. A filly is a young female horse or pony under the age of four. In the early 1800s a wealthy merchant was travelling from Brockenhurst to Lymington to meet a ship coming from the continent. On the way he was set upon by three sailors who murdered him and threw his body into the river. They went to the Filly Inn to spend their ill-gotten booty and the landlord heard them boasting about they had done to the merchant and sent for the militia. They were later found guilty of murder and hanged then gibbetted outside the Filly Inn and their ghosts have been roaming the inn ever since, with much cursing and loud threats.

Fleurs de Lys, Pilley

Built as a pair of cottages in 1096 this is the oldest pub in the New Forest. There is a list of all landlords going back to the fourteenth century. In the pub is a medieval wishing well, a dovecote and pair of ghosts, one of which is a grey-haired woman who frequents the kitchen. The French connection goes back to Norman times when the tract of land was given to William de Vernum and the *fleurs de lys* was part of his armorial bearings. That most splendid of children's books, *The Children of the New Forest*, was published in 1847and the inn is mentioned in it. Carbon testing shows the building goes back to the eleventh century. The two bars are named from Captain Marryatt's book, *Jacob Armitage and Beverley of Arnwood*. The inn was described by Sir Arthur Conan Doyle in *The White Company*. In the original fireplace there is a recess for an hour glass and salt cellars. One previous landlord, himself the son of a previous landlord, traced the pub name back to the coat of arms of William de Vernum who was the landlord owner at the time of King John. The first recorded pub landlord was Benjamin Stones in 1498.

Hyde Tavern, Winchester

This is said to be the oldest pub in Winchester and is haunted by an old woman who pulls clothes off people as they sleep. Sometimes it is a definite tug that awakens the sleeper but sometimes the bedclothes are eased off and found in a different part of the room. Legend has it that it is the ghost of a woman, who was once refused a room here many years ago, and turned away. Later she died of cold as she sheltered nearby. The Hyde is said to have been a pub, or alehouse, when King Arthur reigned in the ninth century.

Old Mill Inn, Holbury

Now here is a magic place to be certain! Off a main road and down a short winding lane, the Old Mill has one of the most picturesque settings in the forest. It is haunted by the earthly spirit of an old monk with a full red beard. It was built in the fifteenth century as a cottage and then a barn added. The oldest part is thatched and covered with ivy while the barn part is now of old red brick. Inside the main bar is an inglenook fireplace with a pile of logs ready for cold nights. The old mill race is now home to goldfish covered with netting against the predatory herons with an old-fashioned dovecote nearby.

Queen's Head, Burley

The inn was built in 1660, at the time of the restoration of Charles II. As an inn it was once the home of smugglers and it is haunted by the ghost of Peter Warne, a well-known local smuggler and highwayman. For some curious and not adequately explained reason, his horse is buried under the pub. It has been maintained that the cellars were large enough to stable horses down there for highwaymen to make speedy forays out onto the roads. Some years ago a secret room was discovered where illicit booty had been stored away from the prying eyes of authority. It has one of the best collections of horse brasses in the country and records of smugglers going back to 1633. At one time there was a local woman, Lucy Warne, who sat up at Picket Post nearby and signalled that the revenue men were about by putting on a red cloak.

Red Lion, Chalton

Originally built as a hostel for builders and artisans working on the local church in 1147, it claims to be one of the oldest pubs in Hampshire and has a licence from 1503. It is thatched with timber framing and stands opposite the village green and the thirteenth-century church. It was a popular stop on the Portsmouth to London coach run. There are two main bars with a huge inglenook fireplace and a bake oven at the side. Brasses, old witches' kettles and other cooking instruments prevail throughout. Ghosts include a woman behind the bar who appears to take an order and then walk away leaving whoever is behind the bar to explain why their drink is not ready, a child playing hide and seek from upstairs down the stairs and into the bar, a face at a top window at closing time and the smell of tobacco from one corner of the inglenook fireplace from a man who died many years ago. Down the road from the pub, on a steep incline, has been seen a spectral horse and cart.

Royal Anchor Hotel, Liphook

Both the pub and village are haunted by exotic apparitions. Highwayman Captain Jacques was caught here by the revenue men and was shot dead as he tried to escape. Since then a man in a tricorne hat with long flowing cloak has been seen. He appears from a large fireplace and is seen to leave through a closed door. Prisoners of war from France were held chained to the walls in the cellars before being moved to secure barracks. A former landlord here, Bob Drake, says he has seen a woman dressed in black bending down and picking up items of clothing on the first floor. The bucolic calm of the village is oft disturbed when the ghost of the White Calf is abroad. It jumps over hedges and charges along the lanes before it finally disappears. Then there is the little Flute Boy who has been seen and heard dancing, singing and playing his flute through the trees and bushes.

Royal Oak, Langstone

As chains are heard rattling in the old stone bar a woman dressed in white has been seen gliding through. Nearby in the village a very tall, thin man with only one leg has been spotted and rumoured to be a passing preacher of long ago. There are also sounds of a chair being dragged along stone tiles in the bar. The inn is over 500 years old and built on the harbour wall. Dogs bark at mysterious sights and some people have felt pressure on their necks while staying here. The Woman in White is thought to have been connected with the bakery that stood next door. Another elderly gentleman, wearing eighteenth-century clothing, has been seen to walk out of the pub, across the main road and then disappear.

Tudor Rose, Fordingbridge

Here, a Cavalier ghost who comes up behind women staff and runs his hands over their hips, is the resident ghost. During the Civil War a Cavalier went to this inn to find his lady friend had been frolicking with other men. He is said to have put a curse on women and, one woman who stayed there, spoke of extraordinary things happening during the night but would never explain. At least 600-years-old this inn is also haunted by footsteps up and downs the stairs. There have also been sightings of a woman gliding up the staircase with the sound of swishing skirts.

Waggon and Horses, Walhampton

Once called the Wagon Ale House it has deeds from 1643, about the time when Charles I had the first English medal struck. It is haunted by a gamekeeper, Henry Card who shot himself in the pub in 1893 when he thought his gun was unloaded. Another gamekeeper had been shot in the back and killed in the nearby woods and foul play was assumed. However, Card demonstrated how a man could shoot himself in the back using his own gun when it went off and fatally wounded him. When Card does appear there is said to be the strong smell of wet tweed.

White Hart Hotel, Andover

A well known coaching inn with a long history of hauntings, the White Hart is at the town centre. A rather exotic Green Lady has been seen gliding (that is the word everyone uses) along a passageway accompanied by the sound of male footsteps. In another part of the inn there has been seen another woman walking with an elderly man. After closing time there is the sound of beer barrels being rolled about in one of the bedrooms and, from time to time, in the yard.

Occasionally a man appears dressed in a leather apron and some people have seen a young girl with him. For some curious reason she only appears in mirrors before she dissolves into a mist. The ground floor is where King Charles I stayed and this is haunted by shadows of a man and a woman.

Royal Anchor Hotel, Liphook

Hertfordshire

Brocket Arms, Ayot St Lawrence

One aged monk from a nearby monastery still keeps his vigil and patrols his earthly patch. The pub and monastery were built about the same time and there is a legend that he was a travelling monk who hanged himself in what is now the bar. Those working at the pub have described him as wearing a long brown garment with a cowl with his head bent forward. Nearby is Shaw's Corner, the home of George Bernard Shaw, playwright and author, for over forty years. An apocryphal tale is told explaining why he moved here. Wandering through the local churchyard with friends he came across a stone dedicated to a woman who died aged ninety-six. The epitaph read, 'Alas her time on earth was short' and Shaw said that that would do nicely for him, too.

Chequers Inn, Anstey

During the seventeenth century this area was noted for the number of brilliant fiddlers. One was Blind George who played at the Chequers Inn. After a night of drinking and merriment they discussed the local Devil's Hole, said to lead by tunnel to Anstey Castle, an eleventh-century building. They said no one went into the cave and came out alive, at which Blind George scoffed. He said he would go in with his dog and return. George went in playing his fiddle and the villagers heard the sound across the fields. Suddenly there was the most awful cry. Minutes later his dog came racing out with all its hair burned off and George was never seen again. Every now and again, across the fields, come the strains of a master fiddler and the dogs in the village whimper. Then a ghostly middle-aged man appears in one of the bars.

Hollybush, Elstree

At this five-centuries-old inn a bearded man with ponderous footsteps has been seen and heard wandering abroad but who suddenly disappears. A nearby car park was once an undertaker's premises and it is thought that some phantoms here are from that occasion. Another man with a Van Dyke type of beard has been seen on many occasions and the story is that he is John Turtle. He was the son of an eighteenth-century mayor, was a heavy gambler and used this inn frequently. He was deeply in debt to another man, William Teare. There was an argument that led to Turtle shooting Teare, cutting his throat and hiding the body in a marsh. Turtle was caught and hanged and Teare was buried in the nearby churchyard. The man with the beard at the Hollybush is said to be William Teare.

White Lion, Walkern

The last claimed witchcraft trial in this country took place in this village in 1712 and the judges and witch-hunters stayed at this inn. By this time it was difficult to get convictions for witchcraft and it finally ceased to be a crime in 1736 although still left on the statute books. However, in this case, Jane Wenham of Walkern was the last witch to be prosecuted and found guilty. She was sentenced to be hanged but was reprieved and had to go into hiding before she was lynched. Since the trial at Walkern there have been reports of cowled men seen in the pub and cries and wailings in the nearby street. But it is not true that it was the last trial under the Witchcraft Act because a woman, Helen Duncan, was tried under that act in 1944. She was a mystic and foreteller of the future and, at séances at Portsmouth, told of British battleships being lost at sea. But no one, even in naval intelligence, knew anything about this. After her trial she was jailed for two years because the Government feared that she could act as a spy for the enemy. This act was finally repealed in 1951.

Right: *Brocket Arms, Ayot St Lawrence*

Below left: *Helen Duncan, White Lion, Walkern*

Below right: *White Lion, Walkern*

Isle of Wight

Hare and Hounds, Downend

Almost 300 years ago Michael Morey, a woodcutter, lived in this village. His grandson inherited an amount of money and Morey fell out with him and attacked him with an axe. The youth died from his injuries and, to hide the evidence, Morey set fire to his cottage. Later the body was found and Morey was arrested and hanged and the body was left on a gibbet opposite this pub. After a while the locals got fed up with this rotting corpse and it was taken down and buried in an unmarked grave nearby. Every now and again he appears outside the inn wearing ragged leather leggings, a jerkin and carrying a huge axe. Some years ago a couple driving from Sandown in rainy weather close to the Hare and Hounds suddenly saw a man in front of their car. The driver braked but both noticed that there was just a skull, rotting clothes and, in his hands, he carried a wooden axe handle. Both screamed out and the apparition disappeared.

Kent

Bell Inn, Hythe

The oldest pub in town, the Bell Inn was the main one when Hythe was a prosperous port. Underneath the floors are tunnels to a millstream used for hiding smuggled goods. In the attic is a hook for a joist to bring in the goods fast. Parts of the inn go back to the fifteenth century and there is a Grey Lady who haunts the cellars and said to have been a former landlady who died giving birth to a child. When the huge inglenook fireplace here was opened up for renovation some years ago the builders found old mugs, clay pipes and a bunch of keys. They also found the bodies of two revenue men who had been murdered and bricked up. It was reported at the time that their uniforms, boots and belts were still in good condition. Some locals maintain that they have seen these two men sitting next to the inglenook fireplace.

Bishop's Finger, Canterbury

In the nineteenth century, many country signposts were made using a pointed finger. This became derisory slang for bishops who can point heavenwards but do not follow their own advice. One woman, Ellen Blean, housekeeper to one canon, found he was having an affair with a younger woman. She poisoned them both with a meat pie and then disappeared. She was later found walled up at a house near this pub and every Friday night her ghost is said to wander this street and appears in one of the front bars of this inn.

Black Horse, Pluckley

At the Black Horse, there are reports of goods going missing on a regular basis only to be replaced in the same position later. The landlord of the Walnut Tree, Aldington, says that a woman he knew was working at the Black Horse who put down her handbag and cardigan in the same place every day. One day they went missing, and, two years later to the day, there was a knocking at the door, although no one was there, and shortly afterwards, the cardigan and bag were found where they had been left previously. The poltergeist here is a woman called Jessie Brooks who was killed in the skittle alley when the pub was in a different part of the village. When it moved she moved with it, almost 200 years ago, and she is seen wandering around looking for a child she lost, according to the legend.

Black Horse, Pluckley

Above left: *Chequers, Doddington*

Above right: *Chequers, Sevenoaks*

Captain Digby, Kingsgate

It is the oldest licensed pub on Thanet and was a former pilgrims' hospice. Digby was a midshipman who served on the *Badger* under Captain McUllock, the first to suppress smuggling in the area when the new coast blockade started in 1816. The pub was once called the Noble Captain Digby. In 1769, the Battle of Botany Bay took place nearby when revenue men ambushed Joss Snelling and his gang as they unloaded their booty. Snelling and four others escaped through an opening in the cliffs. A riding officer was shot on the cliffs and taken back to this pub where he died and still haunts the inn as well as the smuggler, Snelling. This man was born in 1741, and was fined £100 for smuggling at the age of eighty-nine. He died aged ninety-six and had been introduced to the royalty as the 'famous Broadstairs smuggler'.

Chequers, Doddington

Originally twelfth century, it has played a large part in the history of Doddington. It was used by pilgrims going to and from Canterbury and a place where taxes were collected. There are two main bars with a stable door entrance, one fourteenth century and the other fifteenth, which was once four bars, one for each of the social classes. The Chequers is one of the famous haunted pubs of Kent that includes a Cavalier who was killed in an upstairs room and said to be seen peering through an overhanging window. There is also the ghost of a woman, the wife of a previous landlord, heard playing the piano in the private quarters.

Chequers, Sevenoaks

A one bar, old timber framed pub, in a twelfth-century building that used to house the local petty sessions and manor courts in ancient times. There used to be a set of gallows next door to the Chequers and the guilty ones were taken from the cells near the Dorset Arms in Sevenoaks,

Above left: *Cooper's Arms, Rochester*

Above right: *Cricketer's Inn, Meopham*

and were dispatched shortly after their trials. These executions were watched by large crowds and one woman, looking through an upstairs window of the Chequers, saw her son being hanged and dropped dead. Since then she has been seen and heard wandering the premises with occasional cries of anguish. Some years after this event the window was blocked off from public use. The market that is now held outside the pub on Saturday mornings is from the original charter of the thirteenth century.

Cooper's Arms, Rochester

Centuries ago, when this was a priory, a monk was walled up for his secular naughtinesses. This is the oldest pub in Kent, built in the eleventh century and on the site of the Old Priory. Part of the old cellars still remain. Every November the monk reappears to haunt the pub. This aged cleric appears in cowl and gown and walks, groaning. King Henry VIII met his fourth wife, Anne of Cleaves nearby and granted this tavern a coat of arms. The building itself is recorded in the Domesday Book, 1086. There are also tools used by the early monk coopers at the pub.

Cricketer's Inn, Meopham

Said to be oldest formal cricketing inn still existing in the country, it took its name when the Meopham Cricket Club was formed in 1776 and this was their headquarters. As early as 1735 cricket was well established in this village and there was a pub called the Eleven Cricketers, which is the earliest reference to any pub name connected with the game. Before this, the Eleven Cricketers had been called the Swan. The side of the Cricketers is haunted by a woman who hanged herself when her Napoleonic Wars soldier husband returned with a French mistress and the wife appears regularly in the public bar. A local miller, Bob Bennett, a regular at this inn who hanged himself in the nineteenth century, has been seen on the green opposite the Cricketers.

Crown Inn, Shoreham

In her *Companion into Kent*, published in 1934, Dorothy Gardiner tells a story from the nineteenth century. A gang of smugglers appeared at the Crown with a Spaniard who had been wounded. The daughter of Squib the maltster, the landlord, looked after him and then married him and they lived in Shoreham. Later he was press-ganged and, when he returned years later, she had died and he died shortly afterwards. He is said to be the weeping man seen outside the inn. Surrounded by Georgian houses and old cottages, the Crown was built in 1454 and was once made from wattle and daub with a thatched roof.

Dering Arms, Pluckley

An imposing inn that was built as a hunting lodge for the Dering family there is still the ostler's bell for those arriving by horse. There are extremely high and vaulted ceilings throughout and the main bar is heavily beamed and has a flagstone floor. They have their own ghost, an old woman sitting in the bar in Victorian garb. The Dering windows are especially notable at this inn. The parish church is close to the inn and, on a recent visit by the Paranormal Society, curious things happened when they saw and recorded some unusual psychic activity at the church and inn.

George Hotel, Margate

This fine old coaching inn is not as old as the Tudor house across the road from it although it does date from the mid-eighteenth century. It is clear from the adjoining stable and coach house that the George was a main coaching inn in Margate. The hotel was bombed in June 1943 and the present entrance is built into the old-bowed window space. The bedroom above the bar is haunted by a middle-aged woman dressed in the style of the 1940s. She is thought to have been killed in a German air raid over the town.

King's Head, Grafty Green

A classic tale of haunting occurs in this large roadside pub. Many years ago a coach overturned and the driver and passengers were all killed. The party had been on its way to this inn, where they were taken after the accident, and have taken up their ghostly residence here. Tales abound of a coach appearing on misty nights driven by a headless coachman. The King's Head was used as a safe house by Dover Bill, the smuggler. He was almost caught here when surrounded by revenue men during a drinking session. He escaped during the gunfight that followed but several of his men were caught and hanged at Maidstone. Dover Bill was among the thousands who watched the hangings and was ostracised by all who knew him, then, barred from this inn from that day onwards, he died in poverty. He regularly returns outside the pub and appears to be consumed with hatred. There are large murals on the external pub wall of Dover Bill and a coach running by moonlight.

King's Head, Hythe

An old coaching inn it is a large single bar with a number of eating areas. An old-fashioned cooking range, well black leaded, is a feature in the restaurant. It is a low-beamed inn with iron posts supporting the ceiling from when it was, clearly, several bars. There are a number of open fires. It has been an inn since 1513 and was known as the George in 1584, the Sun by 1714 and then the King's Head. On occasions, doors open although they have been locked and bolted. An expert in the supernatural was called in at one time and said it was the ghost of a woman called Catherine Scothers who had been a serving maid at the inn. She died in 1897 and was buried at St Leonards.

Above left: *Dering Arms, Pluckley*

Above right: *Pied Bull, Farningham*

Northern Belle, Mansion Street, Margate

It was named after an American ship, the *Northern Belle* that ran aground in 1857 and foundered on Ness Rock. The *Victory* lugger set sail to help the stricken ship and was struck by a tremendous sea and turned over. All nine crew perished in sight of hundreds of the town's people. Inside the inn are a series of small rooms with a narrow bar, low beams with small pewter pots hanging and a wooden floor. It is haunted by a woman with a very pale face wearing a white shroud. She has been seen in the bar and cellars (once used by smugglers) and was first recorded by landlord, Robert Edward Brockman, in 1869.

Pied Bull, Farningham

A pied bull is an animal of more than one colour and there are several such pubs named this throughout the country. A phantom coach and horses has been heard outside this pub on the main road by people sitting at window seats. This was an old coaching road between London and Dover and the new part of the inn, that incorporates these seats, was once part of the road itself. It was opened in 1612 by Matthias Rage and he stayed there until 1638. In the seventeenth century it was described as, 'A hospicium with barn and garden adjacent'. Between 1780 and 1810, they serviced six coaches a day. In 1710, the licensee was granted a 500- year lease for the water in the garden for the horses.

Red Lion, Lenham

Red Lion, Lenham

Opposite Lenham Square that is frequently used to film period pieces the Red Lion is a fourteenth-century inn surrounded by Georgian and Victorian houses. A ghost, seen here on many occasions, is dressed in seventeenth-century style and thought to be an aged pilgrim. A second ghost here is said to be an earlier landlord. In the bar there is a 1920s style photograph showing an elegant gentleman. It reads, 'Uncle Bert; In the past and in the present'. The word 'present' is written in shivery writing to indicate that uncle Bert is still about the place. This was a resting inn for pilgrims on their ways to and from Canterbury.

Red Lion, Rusthall

At about the time of Cade's Rebellion, when they defeated the royal troops at Sevenoaks, this inn opened its doors as an alehouse and inn for travellers and pilgrims. They claim to have the oldest licence in Kent dating to that period, 1450. The building had been in existence for many years before becoming an inn. There have been reports over the years of ghostly activity with cold spots and noises and, on one occasion the hindquarters of a dog were seen disappearing through a bar door. Customers, who have seen this animal, describe it as a scruffy beast, large and curled up on the floor of the bar. There are also reports of refrigerator doors locking tight. Outside the pub is often heard the clopping sounds of a ghost described as a headless horseman, dressed in armour, and said to look like one of Cromwell's Ironsiders.

Shipwright's Arms, Oare

Out on the edge of the river Swale, this inn is three centuries old and has traces of an earlier building going back to the thirteenth century. It was first licensed in 1738 when George III was born. The landlord sells Goacher's Shipwrecked Ale that may have something to do with the story behind the ghost that haunts the inn. In the nineteenth century, the captain of a ship that sank in the creek on Christmas Eve, managed to pull himself ashore and over the bank that protects the pub. He died of exposure before he was found next day. When he does make an appearance there is the strong smell of rum and tobacco throughout the pub.

Three Cruches, Strood

Almost six centuries old, this weather-boarded and slated-roofed pub has an inn sign showing Crutched Friars who were distinguished by one cross on their backs. The word is a corruption from the Crossed Friars who were of the Holy Cross order. They wore a red cross on their habit and carried a silver cross before them. In the past it has been known as the Three Cruched Friars but a more recent landlord changed this to the Three Cruches, pronounced 'crooches'. At least three ghosts haunt this pub. The landlady said that she, and a large number of staff and local regulars, have seen a well-dressed man wander through the public bar and the dining room then disappear into a wall. 'But it seems quite a harmless old ghost.' she said. Another figure has been seen leaning through a window on the top floor, waving, and laughing.

Walnut Tree, Aldington

Built in the reign of Richard II between 1377 and 1399 it was timber framed, filled with wattle and daub and had a thatched roof until rebuilt. Inside the inn is a bread oven in an inglenook fireplace. There is still a spy hole, once used by the smugglers, to view the marshes searching for revenue men. Cock fighting took place here until 1904 and it is haunted by a man who was killed in the pub during a domestic quarrel and thrown down the well. There have also been reports of phantom children being seen and heard in the bars.

White Hart, Newenden

Opened in the late 1500s with oak beams there is a large inglenook fireplace in the entrance and an ornately carved bench. The White Hart, as a pub name, goes back to the beginnings of the reign of Richard II in 1377 as his heraldic symbol. All of his household staff wore this device and it became a common thing for innkeepers to show their allegiance in this manner, too. It is a two-bar inn with a ghost that haunts the dining rooms. He is said to be dressed as a farmer or farm labourer and occasionally seen sitting at the inglenook fireplace holding an old-fashioned beer mug. There are two bench seats in the inglenook.

Shipwright's Arms, Oare

Three Cruches, Strood

White Horse, Chilham

The white horse is the emblem of Kent and popular as a pub name since the Hanoverians. This White Horse was built as a thatched farmhouse in 1422. It eventually became an alehouse and was used by the church behind it for festivals, weddings and funerals, or arvils, as they were known. Half a century ago, two skeletons were found at this elegant pub and, according to forensic evidence, to have been soldiers killed at the Battle of Chilham in 1381 from Wat Tyler's revolutionary army. An elderly gentleman, in clerical garb, is seen standing at the fireplace with his hands clasped behind his back at 10 a.m. each morning. A former vicar is said to have committed suicide here, many years ago, and comes back to haunt them.

White Horse, Hubert Place, Dover

In 1778, the 25th Foot Regiment, the Edinburgh Regiment, was in the garrison and this pub was named City of Edinburgh after that occasion. It was renamed the White Horse in 1818, after the Kent emblem, and was used to hold inquests during the early 1800s. After one such inquest on a sailor washed ashore, there have been stories since of a man in uniform playing a tin whistle and haunting one of the bars. The original building went up during the reign of Edward III in 1365 when it was occupied by the verger of St James's church, next door. By 1574 it had been taken over by the ale taster for Dover.

Woolpack, Chilham

The pink-washed Woolpack was built in 1422 and has tenancy records going back to 1428 as Joan of Arc took Orleans. Legend has it that a tunnel once connected this inn with Chilham Castle and was wide enough for a coach and horses to drive through to carry prisoners who had been tried at the inn when it was a courthouse. The Woolpack is haunted by a Grey Lady who appears regularly in a front bedroom and who stands beside the fireplace. Once there was a workhouse next door, for the poor and homeless, and it is thought she may have lived there at one time.

Ye Olde Chequers Inn, Tonbridge

On the inn sign is a macabre reminder of summary justice, a hangman's noose. One of the men hanged outside this pub was Wat Tyler's brother after the failed Peasant's Revolt of 1381. Originally built in 1270 now much of it is sixteenth century with original timbers. It is a low-beamed L-shaped bar with brasses and an old yard of ale glass. Many pubs named this were after the money changers' board and who held their business here. The courtyard is said to be haunted by two men dueling with swords. They have been described as fairly young men with plumed hats, close-fitting jackets or tunics and high riding boots.

Lancashire

Q, Stalybridge

The Q has the shortest name of any pub in the country. There was another one, the X at Cullompton in Devon until it became the Merrie Harriers in 1983. The Q is haunted by a little, old woman wearing Victorian clothing and is said to be the great-grandmother of the present landlady. Another ghost at the Q is a labouring man dressed in early 1900s clothing and thought to have been killed working on a local aqueduct. Formerly this was a bakery and a cobbler's shop.

Ye Olde Chequers Inn, Tonbridge

Q, Stalybridge

Star & Garter, Stockport

A most dreadful story lies behind one of the ghosts haunting this town pub. In 1861 a two-year-old boy called George Burgess was seen playing with other children near the Star. Later his murdered body was found in Hempshaw Brook nearby. Over the years the children of the pub's licensees have talked about their 'friend' who comes out to play with them regularly. He is said to be wearing a frock which would be what small boys wore in the nineteenth century. On other occasions a couple have been heard having a row outside a bedroom door. They have been described as wearing old-fashioned clothing who disappear into the wall when they are observed.

Thatched House, Stockport

Originally called the Thatched Tavern the building was the first infirmary in the town and also a mortuary. There are steps down to the mortuary that has been sealed off. This facility had been set up by Dr James Briscall (1751–1814). On occasions he has been sitting at one end of the bar of this pub wearing a high hat of the period. There have been good reports of some people spilling their drinks as they are pushed from behind when no one has been there. The cellar of the pub is home to a female ghost who has terrified those who have come across her.

Leicestershire

White Hart, Ashby de la Zouch

Whenever the licensee here goes down to his cellar he sees puffs of smoke coming from the beer barrels and then sees a young man or girl with their heads hanging to one side. A team of paranormal experts were called in to investigate and a photograph in the bar shows what they call 'energy orbs'. The photographs were checked by Kodak who confirmed that what was pictured was neither dust spots nor film faults. The paranormal team believes the pub is haunted by several apparitions

Lincolnshire

Abbey Hotel, Crowland

Over 150 years ago a local farmer made a bet in this pub he could walk 1,000 miles in the same number of hours. Henry Girdlestone returned to the pub some forty-nine days later having covered 1,025 miles. Since then there have been reports of very tired feet dragging up and down stairs of the hostelry. They say it is old Henry still walking.

Angel & Royal, Grantham

The Angel is one of the oldest inn signs to reflect the connections between inns and travellers or pilgrims. The land on which this stands belonged, originally, to the Knights Templar and in 1212 King John and courtiers held court here. It was at this inn where Richard III signed the death warrant for the Duke of Buckingham in 1483 and Charles I stayed in 1633. When King Edward VII visited the hotel in 1866 it became known as the Angel & Royal. The inn is haunted by a White Lady seen in the bedroom corridors of the second and third floors. In 1707 the then landlord, Michael Solomon, left £2 a year to pay for the preaching against drunkenness on Mayor-making Day and a sermon is preached even now.

Black Horse, Grimsthorpe

The black horse made a good sign for pubs and in the seventeenth century the 'black horse' was the nickname of the 7th Dragoon Guards who had black collars and cuffs and always rode black horses. For years the only people at this inn who saw Gladys, the ghost, were children. But now she has started showing herself to adults. Gladys is said to be the spirit of a woman who hanged herself in the pub many years ago. She is an elderly woman with short, grey and wavy hair. Another ghost has been seen outside the pub wearing a long brown cloak with a hood. From time to time there have been the sounds of a coach and horses pulling up and people talking.

Sun, Saxby

A local man, Tom Otter, got fed up with his wife and killed her with a hedge stake. He was arrested at the Sun Inn when police officers found bloodstains on his clothing. The dead woman's body was taken to the Sun Inn for an inquest. Later, after a trial, he was executed at Lincoln Gaol and the body was taken back to hang outside the Sun Inn to warn other people what could happen to them. As he was being hung in a gibbet the cross bar broke and pitched him into the team of men. The hedge stake, with which he had killed his wife, was kept at the pub for many years. Several times this stake has disappeared from the pub after a mysterious man was seen walking through and, later, found at the scene of the murder.

White Hart Hotel, Lincoln

It must be true; a television programme was made of the ghosts and apparitions that haunt this 600-year-old establishment. In the oldest part of the inn resides the earthly spirit of a child murdered by a rat catcher many years ago. Outside, in the orangery, a ghost highwayman has been seen complete with cloak, tricorne hat and pistol. Other ghosts include a young man who shot himself in unrequited love and an elderly gentleman wearing a smoking jacket and cravat. But, to top it all, there is the apparition of the Ginger Jar Ghost said to wander the third floor hunting for his stolen ginger jar.

London

Anchor Inn, Clink Street, London SE1

One of the last remaining pubs of the Stews of London it was built about the time of Elizabeth I and Samuel Pepys watched the Great Fire of London from here. Clink is the old word for the prison where men women and children were locked up for a wide variety of offences including not being able to pay their debts. At the time of the press gangs, armed naval men, would suddenly descend on such pubs to fill their ships. In one of their raids on this pub they chose a man who had a dog with him that attacked the press gang and one of them slammed a door on it, cutting off the dog's tail. The man was dragged off to serve in His Majesty's Navy and the dog escaped. Since then there have been sightings of the mutilated beast wandering around the pub and howling.

Anchor Tap, Bermondsey, London SE1

Pubs with this name often have a connection with 'anker', a very old name for 8½ galls beer. Every now and again things in the pub appear and disappear and the resident ghost is held responsible. Because he has been around for so long he has been given a nickname, Charlie. One of his larks is to smash all the ashtrays in the middle of the night and play around with the sound systems throughout the pub. On one occasion a woman's watch disappeared from her room and turned up, some eight weeks later, in a laundry basket.

Black Lion, Hammersmith

Angel, Bermondsey Wall, SE16

That hideous lawyer, Judge Jeffreys, still haunts this building from where he used to watch public executions. The ghost of Jeffreys is described as a short, fat man with an unpleasant visage, wearing a black robe and a full-bottomed wig. The Angel pub has been here since the seventeenth century and overlooks the river Thames. It is built out on piles into the river and Execution Dock was nearby. Judge Jeffreys, also known as the Hanging Judge after his trials of officers and men after the Battle of Sedgemoor, tried to escape from another pub, the Town of Ramsgate, across the river, dressed as a sailor. There are also trap doors at the Angel used by river smugglers. The painter Turner was inspired to paint the *Fighting Temeraire* after he saw it being towed to the breaker's yard from the Angel where he was staying.

Angel, St Giles High Street, London WC2

A one-bar city pub it is haunted by a man who was allowed to stop off here for his last drink before being hanged. He refused and went on to meet his maker at Tyburn. What he did not know was that a pardon was on its way and, had he but tarried a while here, he would have lived somewhat longer. Public executions were finally banned in 1868. At one time there were public hangings every six weeks with as many as fifteen criminals at a time. After the hanging there were dreadful fights to get the body for the Surgeon General's Anatomy School and those who wanted parts of the body for good luck or fend off disease. One murderer, William Duell, came back to life as they were about to dissect him two hours after execution and he was sent back to Newgate then later transported to the colonies.

Black Lion, Hammersmith, London W6

Originally this was an heraldic device going back to Owain Glyndwr, the Welsh chieftain, and his father, Madoc ap Meredith, both of whom carried the black lion on their armour and bearings. At this riverside inn a ghost was seen by a rat catcher, a brewer's clerk, a shoemaker's apprentice and the parish warden near the pub in 1803. But the first person to see it was a

Bow Bells, Bow Road, London

pregnant woman. It chased her, gathered her up in its arms and she died of fright two days later. A local man was out walking one night when an excise officer, Francis Smith, looking for this ghost, saw something, fired and shot the nocturnal pedestrian dead. The victim was a builder called Thomas Millwood. At the inquest at the Black Lion the coroner came to a verdict of willful murder and the excise officer, Francis Smith, was committed to the Old Bailey. There he was convicted of murder of Thomas Millwood, but afterwards pardoned. The ghost of Thomas Millwood still walks and there have been reports of sightings over the past few years. In the long room, a small child dressed in Victorian clothing has been seen to skip around the room. She is described as very pretty, about eight-years-old, and dressed like Alice in Wonderland.

Bow Bells, Bow Road, London E3

They treat their ghost here as a feature of the pub and have a warning sign over the door to the ladies' lavatory. This mischievous apparition has been known to flush the loo at most inappropriate times. A number of women, who have reported the 'phantom flusher', say that the door has burst open and a curious force flushes the cistern. One landlord, who saw a strange mist arising from the toilet floor, organised a séance. During this séance there was a loud smash on the door and a window pane shattered.

Flask, West Hill, Highgate, London N6

There is nothing quite like someone being jilted or crossed in love for a ghost to appear. At this eighteenth-century pub a woman wanders about wailing, crying and leaving cold spots behind. There have been stories over the years that it was a young woman who killed herself in unrequited love and there are those who say she is connected with a portrait in the pub. There are those who also believe she is connected with a bullet hole and a bullet in a wall. On occasion she has been seen moving glasses about on tables as though she is having a ouija session and then blowing down the necks of customers.

Above left: *Gatehouse, Highgate Hill, London*

Above middle: *Golden Lion, King Street, London*

Above right: *George Inn, Borough High Street, London*

Gatehouse, Highgate Hill, London N6

Built as an inn about 1306 this was originally a drovers' pub bringing cattle and sheep into the capital. It is set in the middle of the road and was used by graziers and drovers going to Smithfield Market. There is a dummy cupboard built at the pub from which it is said that Dick Turpin escaped from his pursuers on several occasions. It is haunted by Martha, or Mother Marnes, a former landlady who was murdered for her money. The men who robbed and murdered her were never caught. She is often seen in the oldest part of the inn, along with her cat and dressed in black dress with a lace bonnet or hat. But there is one curious feature; she never appears when there are children or animals staying there. Some people have also seen a white-haired gentleman reflected in the mirrors wearing sea-going clothing and staring at them.

George Inn, Borough High Street, London SE1

One of the most famous pubs in London and one of the only surviving coach inns. Built in the fifteenth century it was recorded in 1598 as a pretty dreadful area of slums, brothels, stews and bear and dog fighting. There is legend that Shakespeare took his troupe to act here. It stands on what was one of the main coaching routes out of London and at one time there was up to 100 coaches a week using it. With outstanding black and white frontage it is the last remaining galleried pub in London. The landlord says that often there are strange noises in the night and electric lights going on and off with no one nearby. In 1855 an eccentric local gentleman, George Rymer, hanged himself from the shaft of a wagon and it is said that it is he who has been haunting the courtyard and bars ever since. A former landlady, one Miss Murray, is also still in residence and creates havoc with computers and tills although there is nothing wrong with them when checked by engineers.

Globe Inn, St Saviour's Churchyard, Southwark, London SE1

In March 1807 the stub of a candle dropped in the bar starting a fire that ripped through the old building. The landlord, his wife and five children escaped but five lodgers out of twenty perished in the inferno and smoke. 'Several of the local buildings were much injured' according

Gatehouse, Highgate Hill, London

to newspaper reports. Several of the male lodgers who died have been seen at different times and dressed in old-style clothing and one is described as having a hideously burned face.

Golden Lion, King Street, SW1

There has been a pub on this site for over three centuries. Many pubs are called the Golden Lion and it was the heraldry of King Henry II and the dukes of Northumbria. Over 200 years ago a woman kicked the landlady to death and there have been reports she is still in residence and can be heard shouting. They feature memorabilia from St James Theatre that ran from 1835 to 1957 and, on occasion, two invisible men, said to be actors, have been heard arguing about a missing book.

Grenadier, Wilton Row, London SW1

Set in one of the most salubrious parts of the capital, down some mews, this place is haunted by the ghost of a young Grenadier officer who was caught cheating at cards. He was beaten to a pulp and thrown downstairs to his death. Reports have been made of shapes about the pub along with chills. On one occasion a brewery inspector, a former CID man, was burned on the wrist as though by a cigarette but no one was there. It is also haunted by a man who took his own life by electrocuting himself in one of the bathrooms. The pub was once the mess for the Duke of Wellington's officers. Outside there is a sentry box and the duke's mounting block. A former medium, Trixie Allingham, said a most serious quarrel had taken place here and there was a ghost in the cellar. The pub was once called the Guardsman and said to be most haunted in September when the cheating officer died.

Hand & Shears, Middle Street, EC1

A fine old tavern known locally as the 'Fist and Clippers' it has stood here for over 400 years and was built on the site of a former inn, an alehouse from 1123. The name comes from the cloth merchants at Bartholomew Fair who first set up their stalls in the twelfth century. In the sixteenth century on 24 August, St Bartholomew's Day, the mayor came out of the inn to pronounce the market open and cut the first piece of cloth to be sold with a pair of tailor's shears. From this practice comes the custom of cutting a piece of tape or ribbon on special occasions. Bartholomew Fair ended in 1855. They used to serve condemned prisoners their last pint at this inn on their way to the gallows. One of these convicted men is still about and often heard crying and screaming in the early hours of the morning. One witness said he was wearing a brown suit with a bright neckerchief and had severe head wounds.

Lamb Tavern, Leadenhall Market, EC3

This is a Listed Building from 1780 with a wealth of engraved glass but originally built in 1321 by Sir Hugh Neville and assigned to the mayor of the City of London, Richard Whittington in 1411. A tiled picture shows Sir Christopher Wren with the plans for the monument depicting the Pudding Lane fire that started the Fire of London of 1666. This fire started in the house and shop of Thomas Farynour, the king's baker. He and his family escaped through a window but a maidservant, too scared to climb through, perished. She was the first victim of the fire that raged five days. Later it was rebuilt as a market for butchers and fishmongers. The Lamb was a well-known coaching inn for businessmen visiting shipping offices in Leadenhall Street to make arrangements for shipping goods or themselves abroad. It has been haunted for many years by Old Tom, a nineteenth-century gander that was brought here with 34,000 other geese to be slaughtered. He went on the run and was fed by the local inns. He was reprieved by the butchers who had been hunting for him and left to wander the market. Old Tom died in 1835 and lay in state for some time. He can still be heard honking inside the Lamb and there is also the occasional sound of crackling fire and people screaming.

Market Porter, Stoney Street, London SE1

One of the oldest pubs in Southwark it has been here since 1638 and one of the few still open in the morning for market porters. They have an up-market ghost who stands at the bar demanding cigars in a loud voice, but, when staff turn around, he has gone. Regularly they have trouble with the place settings in the restaurant and cutlery is moved around or disappears. The landlord has found the till ringing up amounts after it had been emptied. On another occasion after he had turned off the glass-washing machine he found in the morning it had been turned back on and water flooding the pub.

Old Nun's Head, Nunhead Green, London SE

First licensed in the reign of King Henry VIII it is one of the oldest pubs in London. It was built on the site of a nunnery suppressed by the same king. The King's Commissioners went to the Mother Superior and gave her an order of expulsion and she resisted the intruders. During the rumpus she was murdered and her head left on a pikestaff on the nearby green 'For all to see and tremble at the might of the zealous monarch'. Another tale is that she had been caught kissing the King and had been murdered to keep her quiet. Since 1971 there have been reports of swishing curtains in the saloon bar and a pale-faced nun dressed in black apparel appeared. She was the Mother Superior, Elizabeth Barton, recognised from early portraits. A conference room left unlocked was later found locked up and an ancient iron key left in the lock. A locksmith said it would be impossible to lock the door with that key because it was so brittle it would snap.

Above: *Hand & Shears, Middle Street,
London*

Right: *Hand & Shears, Middle Street,
London*

Lamb Tavern, Leadenhall Market, London

Old Queen's Head, Essex Road, London N1

The old inn on this site was used for some time by Sir Walter Raleigh when he was in London. Although that original inn has long gone the present one is haunted by a woman in Tudor dress and a small unhappy little girl. Every first Sunday in the month there is most curious happening. The doors of the pub are opened and then closed although no one is about and then there is the sound of footsteps going away from the inn. Queen Elizabeth I stayed here at the same time as the Earl of Essex. There is also the sound of the swish of a long dress and merry laughter and occasionally is seen a woman wearing Tudor-style dress. Many of the Queen's Head signs throughout the county used to be of Elizabeth I. From time to time she was not best pleased with these portraits of herself and caused them to be pulled down and burned. This was by Royal Proclamation of 1563 and any future designs had to be approved by Her Majesty.

Opera Tavern, Catherine Street, London WC2

This really is a *Phantom of the Opera* pub designed by Jonathon Treacher, in 1879. It is used by singers from the Theatre Royal. Nearby is an alleyway used by Charles II for assignations with Nell Gwynne. The actor, Richard Baddeley, who died there in 1794, haunts it and there is a room named after him. Over the years has been heard a rich, actorial voice declaiming and sights of him in a long, dark cloak. Baddeley first appeared in 1761 and, a huge success in low comedy, made a fortune. When he died he left property to fund a home for 'decayed actors' and £3 a year for wine and cake in the Green Room at the Theatre Royal on the twelfth night of Christmas.

Opera Tavern, Catherine Street, London

Tabard, Chiswick, London W4

The tabard was a short-sleeved surcoat decorated with the coat of arms of a knight and worn over the armour to show his identity and often connected with pilgrim pubs. The tabard was first used in Palestine to keep the heat off the knights' armour. Chaucer and his pilgrims set off for Canterbury from another Tabard inn in south-east London that burned down in 1676. The Tabard, Chiswick, is a well-known pub with a renowned theatre. It has been haunted since the late-nineteenth century by an elderly woman. Often she is seen sitting at a table in the bar dressed overall in black. She appears to be whistling but those who have seen her say no sound comes from her.

Volunteer, Baker Street, London NW1

This was at one time a manor house belonging to the Neville family. One of the ancestors, Robert Neville, who was a Cavalier during the English Civil War fought at the Battle of Naseby in 1645, and still 'lives here' and his ghost is seen on many occasions. He is seen in the cellar wearing breeches, stockings and a surcoat. The Volunteer was built on the site of the Neville house that had been burned out in a fire that killed all the members of that family. The name 'volunteer' used in pub names usually refers to volunteer regiments who went to do battle with Napoleon in France and other wars. (It is just down the road from 221B Baker Street, the reputed home of the literary character, *Sherlock Holmes*).

Warrington Hotel, Warrington Crescent, London W9

One of the most opulent inns of London it was a brothel when owned by the Church of England in the late 1800s. Built in 1859 and refurbished in 1900 it has most outstanding pub architectural features. The smaller bar is of elegant stucco and small, etched glass windows. Music hall star Marie Lloyd used this bar when quaffing champagne with admirers and said to still haunt the place. One of her empty champagne glasses still adorns a mantelpiece in the lounge bar. Early in the 1900s a champion jockey rode his winning horse up over the steps and into a bar where he quaffed champagne. Even now the ghost of a whinnying horse and cheering voices can be heard from this bar.

White Hart, Gunthorpe Street, London E1

On the corner of Gunthorpe Street and an eerie alleyway this pub was known to Jack the Ripper and his victims. A notice on the wall says it is haunted by a woman dressed in Victorian-style clothing and weeping. One of the Ripper's victims, Martha Turner, had her last drink here before being murdered. George Chapman, a barber-surgeon who lived in the cellars of this pub, was arrested as a suspect for the ripper murders and later hanged. (Well, he had poisoned three wives, but was he Jack the Ripper?) Chapman has been heard shouting in the cellars and some claim to have seen him dressed in late-Victorian dress. Built in 1721 it became infamous after Dick Turpin shot dead a law officer after being tracked down to the White Hart in 1739.

William 4th, Hampstead, London NW3

There are two ghosts at this pub set in fashionable Hampstead. One is that of a young girl wearing a long white dress or nightgown with long hair in plaits and a most unhappy face. She can be seen looking through the windows on the first floor and the story is that she committed suicide in a dental surgery that was opposite the pub. The other ghost is said to have lived at the pub many years ago who was murdered by her husband and walled up. She ensures that people know she is still about by loud wailings with the shaking of windows and banging internal doors during the night.

Warrington Hotel, Warrington Crescent, London

White Hart, Gunthorpe Street, London

Ye Olde Cock Tavern, Fleet Street

Ye Olde Cock Tavern, Fleet Street, EC4

Another previous home from home to journalists this pub is haunted by Oliver Goldsmith, the Irish playwright. Ye Olde Cock boasts a fireplace reputed to have been carved by Grinling Gibbons, the world-famous wood carver. There is a picture of Oliver Goldsmith on the first floor and, because of this, a woman was able to identify him in a terrifying haunting. She said she was working in the bar and suddenly, before her very eyes, was a grinning head at the back door. It was that of Goldsmith and since then others have reported sights of him with more of his body showing each time. Goldsmith is buried in the church of St Mary, nearby.

Middlesex

Bell Inn, Hounslow

Hounslow Heath was one of the most notorious places for people being held up and robbed in past centuries. At one time there were rows of gibbets holding hanged highwaymen and people used to coach out from London just to see them. Then they started exhibiting the bodies of the hanged men outside the Bell Inn. One seems to have taken up residence in the pub and has been seen on many occasions. From time to time, barrels of beer that have been locked in the cellar have been smashed open although no one has been near them. One bar cellarman tells of a dreadful experience in the cellar when he came face to face with the image of just a head and shoulders, with a rope around its neck.

Norfolk

Duke's Head, King's Lynn

More than four-centuries-old this was an important coaching inn for stages between Yarmouth, Norwich and London. Over the years there have been tales of a woman dressed in sixteenth-century costume wandering the inn and weeping. It is maintained that this is the earthbound spirit of Margaret Read, a local witch, who had been employed at the hotel and poisoned her mistress in 1590. Legend has it that she was boiled to death in a large cauldron in Tuesday Market Place, nearby. At one point her heart burst from her body and flew through the air into the wall where the mark can still be seen.

Goat Inn, Brundall

There was a once a goat's head on the wall of this 400-years-old inn. It was taken down and locked in a shed but then kept reappearing in the pub. This was said to be the Devil himself. Unfortunately history does not record its final resting place. Mirrors fall off walls and the piano starts playing music when no one is near it. Even the juke box turns on and plays music without a record on the turntable. Water drips through a ceiling with no signs of any flooding above. It is said to be haunted by a Royal Navy man who was killed during the Second World War who had been a customer at the pub.

Hall Inn, Sea Palling

A psychic investigation group moved in here some thirty years ago to check on the stories about haunting in the pub. They used what was, at the time, sophisticated equipment, and picked up strange sounds and other information that suggested something was afoot. It was thought at one time the ghost was that of a Mary Cubbitt but the team decided on the information they received that it was that of another local woman, Kitty Taylor. On several occasions a woman dressed in grey has been seen sitting on the window sill of the television room with a freezing temperature drop in the room. There has also been the overpowering smell of a strong tobacco in bedrooms. On one occasion the landlady saw a column of grey smoke move across the dining room to the kitchen

King's Head, Hethersett

An old-fashioned inn with clay tiles and beams it has a sad tale behind it. Many years ago four bridesmaids were murdered nearby and still haunt the area. They were on their way back from a wedding to this inn when the dreadful deed took place. At first it was thought to have been an accident because the coach was found in a deep pond. Later evidence showed it had been a robbery by at least one highwayman. When the apparition is seen all four are headless as is their coachman as they wander through the lanes outside the pub.

Scole Inn, Scole

Probably one of the most impressive old coaching inns of this county it was built over 350 years ago. It still has the imposing archway through to the old courtyard and inside oak beams and doors and a carved staircase. Over the years the ghost of a woman called Emma, who had been murdered there by her husband, has appeared on a number of occasions and always weeping. She was alleged, by him, to have been unfaithful. Guests at the Scole have included Charles II, Lord Nelson and an infamous highwayman, John Belcher. When pursued by the authorities he rode his horse up the great staircase and escaped from the top floor. Sounds of clattering hooves are often heard in the old courtyard and inside the inn. In a local house near this inn some local people pursue psychic experiments where they claim to have had 'apports', which is a physical transfer from one dimension to another. They maintain that some had come from the Scole Inn.

Victoria, Happisburgh

A gem of a pub of bucolic excellence with camping facilities for walkers. But over 300 years ago this pub was the centre of smugglers and there is legend of a mad spectre. When it appears there is a body of a man without legs and a head hanging down over his shoulders. It leaves the pub and goes out to sea with a large bundle. It then returns and disappears into the ground at Well Corner. For several nights local people watched this apparition put articles down the well and then they decided to search it by daylight. They found a large sack with a man's body in it. They say the phantom was a smuggler who came to an untimely end at the cutlasses of his enemies.

Northamptonshire

Bell at Finedon, Finedon

This is the oldest pub in Northamptonshire dating from about 1042 and said to be the third oldest in the country. In one niche of the frontage is a statue of Queen Edith, wife of Edward the Confessor. At one time there was a carved plaque of Queen Edith hanging inside the Bell that read, 'Queen Edith; Lady, once of Finedon, Where at the Bell good fare is dined on', which would date it at about 1042. Gables at the rear of the inn has a date-stone of 1598. Over the years there have been stories of a strange old man lurking in the stone-carved doorway who disappears when spoken to. Some have reported him as wearing an old-fashioned smock; others have him as him wearing a piece of farm sacking around his shoulders to make a short cloak.

Black Lion Inn, Northampton

For years a poltergeist has reigned here. Lights go on and off and beer barrels are moved about in the cellar. Following a strange mist that seeps through the pub there have also been rattling doors. One night a landlord went to his bedroom and, standing in the room, was a man with a large dog. He thought it was a thief and shouted, 'Get out of here. Who are you?' and both apparitions disappeared. A local psychic research group went over the pub and reported a curious flickering light in the cellar and the sound of a baby crying. What then transpired was that a former owner of the building, Andrew McRae, had been hanged for killing his mistress and their baby here many years ago. The local belief is that both mother and baby are still in residence. There have also been phantom footsteps following people and whispering to them.

Ship Hotel, Oundle

At this six-centuries-old town pub there are said to be two ghosts, both haunting the bedrooms. Over twenty years ago the pub was closed for three years and ghost hunters offered to stay here and cleanse the place of its indwells but were unsuccessful. One previous landlord here killed himself by jumping from an upstairs window. Something brushes past people as they go up the stairs. One room is described as 'disturbing' and people do not like sleeping there. The ship is one of the oldest inn signs in history and was associated with the biblical Ark.

Talbot, Oundle

The building itself is probably 1,200 years old and was at one time a monastery hospice. It was originally known as the Tabret, which meant an hospitium. Over 300 years ago a former landlord

Above left: *Bell at Finedon, Finedon*

Above right: *Ye Olde Cross, Alnwick*

took away stones from the demolished Fotheringhay Castle where Mary Queen of Scots, stayed before her execution in 1587. Her executioner stayed at this hostelry the previous night where he dined on pigeon pie. Part of the castle staircase was used in the rebuilding and since then terrible sobs and cries have echoed around the pub. A portrait of Queen Mary fell off a wall during a discussion about her. Photographers have tried to snap the haunted parts but their films have come out blank. Guests and staff here have heard a woman wailing and keening in one bedroom, which has always been empty at the time. One gentleman, on his way to his room, heard footsteps behind him and turned to find nobody there. One guest saw and spoke to a woman who was wearing a fawn-coloured dress with a white blouse and small cap. She was also wearing an apron or pinafore over the dress and thought to have been a maid. When she spoke to her the apparition just faded away. The ghost has also been seen down in the yard from a window on the landing.

Northumberland

Ye Olde Cross, Alnwick

A most terrible curse was laid on this well-known town pub. Over 200 years ago a former landlord was putting his bottles of beer into the window for show. He keeled over with a severe heart attack and before he died put a curse on the bottles and said that anyone touching them would follow his untimely demise. The bottles have remained untouched since in the window since then and locally the pub is known as 'Dirty Bottles'. His unhappy spirit still haunts the inn with the rattle of glass on glass and foul oaths.

Ye Olde Trip to Jerusalem, Nottingham

Nottinghamshire

Nag's Head, Mansfield Road, Nottingham

As a tradition it was usual for criminals on their way to be hanged at the hill top, to drop in at this old coaching inn for their last drink of Nottingham ale. One of them refused this tempting offer and was taken to his execution. Three minutes later his reprieve arrived. There are stories of poltergeist activity with machines rocking backwards and forwards with lights going out and a chair moving across a room with no one nearby. The last man to be publicly hanged, after a visit to the Nag's Head, was William Wells in April 1827 for highway robbery.

Ye Olde Ramme, Mansfield

This four-centuries-old inn had connections with the wool trade, hence its name. It is said there was a secret tunnel between the inn and a local priory. The Olde Ramme is haunted by at least two monks who have been seen wandering about during the daytime. Some years ago renovation work was done and revealed the wattle and daub of the original tavern. Prior to that, again during renovation work, a seventeenth-century clothes press was found. In 1817, a girl trying to find work in Mansfield, was murdered by a scissors grinder, Charles Rotherham. He tried to sell her few possessions in Ye Olde Ramme and was arrested and later hanged. Her ghost still appears on occasion at the inn and at a memorial stone dedicated to her.

Ye Olde Salutation, Nottingham

An ancient inn it was once called the Archangel Gabriel Saluting the Virgin Mary. This upset the Puritan zealots and the landlord was obliged to change it to the Soldier and Citizen. This was again changed in 1660 on the return of the Royalists. During the Civil War the pub was used as a recruiting centre for both Cavaliers and Parliamentarians. The date, 1240, appears on the outside of the inn dating the first building on the site and there is a carbon timber date of 1360. Beneath the foundations are hewn-out caves which were thought to be storage cellars but were investigated and shown to be a Saxon settlement. These caves are haunted by a girl aged about four or five and thought to be a street urchin who came to an untimely end.

Ye Olde Trip to Jerusalem, Nottingham

Hewn into the rock of the castle above this is another claimant for the oldest inn in the country. Painted on the outside is the date 1189 and is said to date from the time of the crusades to the Holy Land. There are caves and passageways behind the pub that has become world famous. Behind the pub cellar is Mortimer's Hole named after a man who was executed and still haunts the caves and the bars. Local legend has it that the pub started out life as the Pilgrim but what is certain is that the building is of very great age. One of the oldest and most famous fairs, the Goose Fair, is held in Nottingham every year. Nottingham was an Anglo-Saxon settlement known as Snotingham, meaning the hamlet of Snot's People. The reason it became Nottingham was because the Normans could not pronounce 'sn' and the 's' was dropped.

Oxfordshire

Barley Mow, Clifton Hampden

A most attractive inn thatched, low built and dated on the outside of the white- washed wall as 1352. Mentioned by Jerome K. Jerome in his *Three Men in a Boat* each bedroom for guests is named after a character from that book. In the thatched roof there are breeding doves. Two centuries ago one Sarah Fletcher lived in one of the great houses nearby and hanged herself in 1799 because of her cruel husband. She is seen wandering the road outside this pub, and occasionally in one bar of the Barley Mow and in the meadows near the river. She is always wearing a purple ribbon in her auburn hair and weeping.

Bird Cage, Thame

During the Napoleonic Wars it was used to billet French prisoners of war and was known locally as the 'Bird Cage'; this, eventually became the inn name. It was also used as a magistrates' court with stocks outside. At one time, a man thought to be a leper, was stoned to death in the

Barley Mow, Clifton Hampden

pub and can be heard beating on doors to get out. Curious and fearful sounds are heard on the winding staircase between 2.30 and 3 a.m. One unbeliever in phantoms, ghosts, indwells, wraiths and the like, said so, loudly in the bar, and a pot flew off the wall and struck the licensee on the head. 'It came off and straight into her as though by an invisible hand' one observer noted. There is also some history of a tunnel between the Bird Cage and St Mary's church, Thame. That church is haunted by a Grey Lady who first appeared in 1903 when a vicar was preparing for communion.

Bull, Henley on Thames

At this town pub there have been reports of the odour of candles in one bar. One night a man staying there awoke to find a cowled figure bending over him as he lay abed. At the nearby Kenton Theatre a play, *The Hanging Wood*, was being produced here some thirty years ago. The play, about a girl who was hanged for poisoning her father at the Little Angel, Remenham, in 1752, ran into the most curious difficulties during rehearsal. Mirrors leapt off walls, lights were turned on and off and doors opened and closed with no one nearby. Then there was the figure of a young girl who appeared at the back of the theatre only to disappear when spoken to. When a member of the cast mentioned the name 'Mary Blandy', the girl who was hanged, a cup lifted several inches from a table and crashed to the ground.

George Hotel, Dorchester on Thames

An unhappy soul, another White Lady, has been seen here at this most ancient of pubs. She usually appears at the end of a four-poster bed in one room and weeping. The present building is dated 1449 but there has been an inn here since 1140. The galleried quarters for the nearby priory hospice are the oldest in the country. It was at one time an important coaching inn between London and Oxford. One is reminded of this by the eighteenth-century carriage that is kept outside the inn.

George Hotel, Dorchester on Thames

Hopcroft's Holt, Steeple Aston

Claude Duval was a notorious highwayman who appears on this inn sign. He came to England from France and was footman to the Duke of Richmond before he turned to highway robbery. At one time he was on the most wanted list of highwaymen and then fled abroad where he pretended to be an alchemist and managed to con a number of people out of their gold and jewellery. He was finally captured back in London but, although armed to the teeth, was too drunk to fight back. In 1670 he was hanged by Jack Ketch and later his body finished up in Surgeon's Hall. Later he was buried at Covent Garden. His ghost is said to haunt this pub where he is known to have planned and committed some of his crimes. The inn is also haunted the ghosts of a previous landlord and his wife who were both murdered here. There are also good reports of ghostly Cavaliers and the sound of voices during the night when no one is about.

King's Arms, Holywell Street, Oxford

The site of this town pub was once part of a religious house and its first licence as an inn was granted almost four centuries ago. The first time *Hamlet* was performed in public was at this pub courtyard by strolling actors. Over many years, two elderly men have been heard chattering in one of the small bars but they have remained invisible. A classics undergraduate, who worked here as a barman, said they were speaking in ancient Greek and they were discussing the relative qualities of port. At one point they become quite excited and then there is the sound of a blow and the discussion runs out of steam. As a university, Oxford was set up in AD 727 when St Frideswide and twelve colleagues started a monastic centre of religious learning and grammar.

Old Crown Coaching Inn, Faringdon

Built in 1664 this inn was also a magistrates' court under that evil jurist, Judge Jeffreys. On one occasion he had fourteen men hanged in the courtyard. One of those hanged was an innocent man. The good burghers of Faringdon went after the hangman who took refuge at this inn. They threatened to burn

77

King's Arms, Holywell Street, Oxford

Old Crown Coaching Inn, Faringdon

him out after the soldiers guarding him had left and he leapt to his death. Then there is Nancy who bore a bastard child to another innocent man who had been hanged. She threw baby and herself from the roof in her extreme grief. As one would expect, this inn is not just home to one restless spirit, but several. Two women have been heard crying and trying to comfort each other.

Plough, Upper Wolvercote
Once it was a very rough pub indeed when it was used by bargees and navigators at the start of the 1800s. In a dreadful accident on Christmas Eve, 1874 a train from Paddington to Birkenhead was very crowded and there was ice on the track. After Kidlington it started rocking seriously and at the canal bridge a wheel collapsed and thirteen coaches tipped over. Some thirty-four people were killed and more than 100 severely injured and they were taken by farm carts to the Plough. The stables were used as a hospital and temporary morgue. Ever since that date there have been stories of ghosts at the inn and sounds of terrible groaning.

Tite Inn, Chadlington
A strange name for a pub and there is nothing like it in the dictionary. It is thought to derive from old name for an ancient water spring. The pub was built in the 1600s and is haunted by an elderly woman, always seen in the cellars. She is dressed in very old-fashioned garb and is thought to be connected with the Battle of Edgehill that took place in 1642. A special investigation into belief in witchcraft was carried out in the area before the First World War and many local people said they believed in it. They claimed that in living memory, (then) three witches had been buried alive with only their heads above ground.

Weston Manor Hotel, Weston on the Green
In the Middle Ages there was a somewhat jaundiced view of monks and nuns romping together. Two such church folk were caught in *flagrante delicto*. She was burned at the stake near this inn

while he was ex-communicated. Apart from the phantom coach and horses seen and heard outside, one room at this inn is haunted by the earthly spirit of the nun, known as Mad Maude. There have been reports of hauntings in the Oak Room over the years and a reporter from the British Tourist Board spent a night there. He slept badly because of the most unusual heat in Maude's room. It is a fourteenth-century building and there are good reports of ghostly coaches and horses arriving in the middle of the night and running over cobblestones.

White Hart Inn, Minster Lovell
A teenager is heard sobbing and crying at this fifteenth-century former coaching inn. She is known as Rosaline and wears a misty veil. There have been glasses disappearing from the bar with weeping sounds in the background A hand bell, used in the pub to call time, has been set off well before drinking up time. On one occasion a barrel was knocked off its stand in the cellar and they blamed a poltergeist. The first Viscount Lovell hid out at Minster Lovell Hall helped by an aged retainer. This gentleman died before he could get help for the viscount who starved to death in his hiding place, only to be discovered in 1708.

Shropshire

Feathers Hotel, Ludlow
Several people have seen the ghost of a young woman in modern dress, including a miniskirt, cross the road to this inn and disappear through the wall from the pavement. A commercial traveller saw the figure of a young girl with a see-through blouse and short skirt come out the hotel and disappear into the pavement. He ran inside, white and shaking, and was told 'It's all right. You have seen a young girl disappear into the pavement. Have a brandy, it's on the house'. It now takes a very curious turn. In the early 1980s a reporter tracked down the 'ghost'. She was then in her twenties and still alive. She used to visit her aunt, a Mrs Hughes, who lived near the Feathers. After the aunt died this woman used to visualise herself walking from the Feathers to her aunt's home and, finally, this became a curious reality. The Feathers is a 300-year-old former coaching inn.

Somerset

Bird in Hand, Glastonbury
About 100 years ago a landlord died in a fire after falling asleep holding a glass of cider and a cigar. He has been wandering about ever since. Staff have come across the old gentleman when about their duties in the cellars when he has given them a sharp tweak with cold air blown on the neck. Most of the trouble started after a licensee knocked down a wall in the pub while refurbishing and glasses started flying around and mirrors dropping off wall hangings.

Castle Hotel, Castle Green
That ubiquitous jurist, Judge Jeffreys, stayed at this former castle when he was at his most savage against the followers of the Duke of Monmouth during the rebellion of 1685. Here there is the fiddler's room where, from time to time, music has been heard played on a violin. Some people have described seeing this musician and she is said to be wearing evening dress from the early-twentieth century. They have also maintained they have seen Judge Jeffreys in the hotel and in the town, gnawing on a large meat bone.

Chough Hotel, Chard

The chough is the name which describes several types of crow. However, it usually refers to the red-legged crow which is found on sea cliffs in Cornwall. Old legend has it that when King Arthur died his spirit became a chough and flew away. Three different phantoms are said to frequent this inn. One a man in a suit of armour, another of a man with a vinegary visage and one aged crone. There is also the remains of a bird in a small coffin included in the pub inventory. There is a tombstone at the back of the fireplace that has defied all efforts to photograph it. On refurbishment a small room was found that no one knew about. It seemed to be a small powder room for ladies and part of a bedroom wall that had appeared to be solid and there are sounds of female laughter coming from this room and girls whispering. Some people claim to have been attacked with either a rod or whip as they lie cowering in bed and have marks on their body the following day. Carbon testing at this pub shows the building to be 1,200 years old. One police officer visiting saw an old man by the fire drinking from an old-fashioned mug. There have been incidents when glass pint pots have leapt from the bar but do not break.

George & Pilgrim, Glastonbury

To this day Glastonbury remains the spiritual centre of England. Longstanding rumours are that the Holy Grail was buried in the man-made mound over 550-ft high. Nearby was the Benedictine abbey where two unknown chapels were discovered earlier this century and said to have been found by mystic means. Christianity is said to have been brought here by Joseph of Arimathea who had put Jesus's body in his own grave in Palestine. Glastonbury is also reputed to be the fabled Isle of Avalon. The George & Pilgrim was built in 1475. A monk has been seen on many occasions at the inn. A more modern ghost, dressed in blue, has been seen sporting a wide and happy smile.

George Inn, Wedmore

An elderly woman dressed in Edwardian-style attire has been seen to appear here in mirrors. She has also been seen in some of the corridors and to then disappear into the wall. There is also a mean-minded apparition that holds people down in bed. A poltergeist has been active and a cup has suddenly started turning around on its own on several occasions. This is an inn over 500-years-old and has part of the old churchyard and graveyard in the foundations. One customer saw an apparition in the mirror of his bedroom one night. He looked behind him, thinking it was an hotel servant, but there was no one there. When he turned again to look in the mirror she was there behind him and looking at him intently. She was dressed in Edwardian-style clothing with a high-necked blouse and long black hair streaked with grey. The woman has also been seen attending Christmas parties at the inn and always wearing a long, black dress.

Holman Clavell Inn, Blagdon Hill

A phantom player has been heard in the skittle alley of this 600-year-old pub. Items have disappeared from rooms and a beer jug filled itself up during the night. In one case a book went missing from the bar counter and found thirty days later in a wardrobe upstairs. Now, who is responsible for all this mayhem and disaster, but Chimbley Charlie. This horror sits above the fireplace on a beam made of holman, the dialect word for holly and the beam is the clavey or clavvy. On one occasion a farmer, who had made mock of Charlie, organised a party at the inn. But a maid who was setting tables said to the farmer, 'Charlie don't like 'ee.' When a check was made this hearth demon had cleared the table set for supper, all the tankards were hung up and linen cleared and folded. They took this as a sign Charlie did not want the farmer there and the party was cancelled.

Staffordshire

Royal Oak Inn, Abbots Bromley

A small town with a most impressive history and an annual horn dance. A guest staying at the Royal Oak some years ago went into an attic room by mistake and saw a white figure. It was an old man with a very large and bushy beard. The guest backed out of the room and went to tell the licensee about what he had seen. A group of people went up into the attic and searched it but found nothing; the old man had just disappeared. Some weeks later the landlady woke up in the night and saw a tall man in a long cloak going into the bathroom. From time to time a fireplace in the bar emits strange musical sounds at any time of day and night.

Whittington Inn, Kinver

A fourteenth-century inn that was once the home of Dick Whittington, thrice Mayor of the City of London. It is haunted by Lady Jane Grey, who spent time here as a child. She was Queen of England for only a few days until arrested and executed by Mary Tudor, legal claimant. On one occasion an employee took a bull mastiff to his room and some nocturnal visitor terrified the beast out of its mind. One guest awoke here to find that something was pushing down on his legs. Then this pressure was moved up to his throat and he was unable to move or scream. Gradually the pressure gave up on him and he fled from the room. A mysterious altar was found in the attic above that room. There is also the legend of the cowled monk who makes an occasional appearance. One man lashed out at a figure bending over him and banged his fist straight into a wall. Sir Richard Whittington was born at Pauntley Court, Gloucestershire, in the fourteenth century. The legend is that he made a fortune by his cat, Miss Puss, who was an absolute power in the mouse-hunting world. But the story of his cat came much later because, during his lifetime, he had an engraving of him with his hand on a skull. The good burghers of London City did not like this and it was changed to a cat. Of such whims are legend made. He died in 1423. The real story of Whittington's 'cat' was that this was the name for the barges that brought thousands of tons of coal into the capital and landed along the present Embankment on the north side.

Whittington Inn, Kinver

Suffolk

Angel Inn, Lavenham
Without a doubt one of the most beautiful and best-preserved medieval towns in the country. Its riches came from the wool trade over several centuries and shows in the wealth of architectural detail in the town. The Angel got its first licence in 1420. This splendid inn is haunted by a little old lady dressed in old-fashioned clothing. On one occasion the landlady went to open up the pub at Christmas time and saw the old lady staring at the Christmas tree. She just smiled to the landlady and then disappeared. She is said to be the spirit of a Mrs Goodhew, a former landlady.

Bell Inn, Walberswick
For over 400 years there have been tales of the Devil haunting this pub in the shape of a black dog. A large beast, it has also been seen to haunt the road between the pub and the local vicarage. Records tell of invisible horses galloping across the common and a small man dressed in brown seen to enter the churchyard only to disappear. During the eighteenth century a Negro drummer called Toby, from a local regiment, murdered a Walberswick girl. He was caught and hanged and since then there have been stories of an apparition coach driven by a black coachman in the lane near where he was executed. George Orwell, (as the young Eric Blair), saw a large black dog apparition that runs across the marshes at low tide. As far back as 1577 local people talked of the Devil's dog about the size of a calf. Blair also saw a man, small and stooping, outside the church and followed the man to the pub where he disappeared into a wall.

Bull, Long Melford
For many years this building, six-centuries old, was hidden under a Georgian frontage. When it was renovated over sixty years ago its original splendour of timbering was revealed. One of the timbers is carved as a 'woodwose', a wild man of yore who roamed the county and appears in much of its mythology. Over 400 years ago a man was murdered at this pub and his killer went to the gallows. Now both of them still haunt the place. In one curious incident a number of dining-room chairs were found grouped around the fireplace as though there had been a number of people sitting there although they had not been arranged thus the previous night. In another incident a small fire started on a carpet almost 6ft away from a fireplace which was not in use at the time.

Crown Hotel, Bildeston
Here there is said to be at least four phantoms. One is a woman in a grey costume seen in the stables where she is said to have hanged herself, an aged gentleman in a tricorne hat, and two children in ragged, Victorian-style dress holding a music box. Throughout the village there are stories of people being touched as they sit drinking in the pub and strange footsteps and banging late at night. A local policeman took on an investigation here some forty years ago but all to no avail; he found no conclusive evidence. The inn was built in 1495. A journalist who stayed here in room fifteen, left his towels neatly piled on top of the chest of drawers but, when he returned, they had been thrown untidily across the bed. During the night he was awakened several times by weird wailing sounds. A suicide in one room took place many years ago and in another room a woman was strangled.

*Nutshell, Bury
St Edmonds*

Nutshell, Bury St Edmunds

A plaque outside this attractive pub claims it to be the smallest in the country. It is said that eight to ten people inside will fill it. But, in 1984, 101 men and a dog were squeezed into it. Every now and again the ghost of a small boy appears in the tiny bar and is said to be that of a lad murdered at the inn many years ago. He is seen standing at the end of the bar with a most unhappy face.

White Hart, Blythburgh

Once the local courthouse, the White Hart has a large oak door inside the main entrance. From time to time there have been furious bangings on it and local legend has it that it is the ghost of a monk from a nearby religious establishment. Apart from that there are reports of a coach and horses rattling past on the way to Walberswick and the ghost of Toby, a black soldier drummer hanged for the murder of a local girl, driving it. Tobias Gill a drummer in the Dragoons had been thrown out the White Hart one night for drunkenness. He met Ann Blakemore and raped and murdered her, then passed out near her body. There is still a local field named after him, Toby's Walk.

Ye Olde Three Tuns, Bungay

This has to be almost top of the list for the number of ghosts and apparitions wandering about in any inn. They claim to have at least twenty different ones. Some seem to lay dormant for years and then make their presence felt. The most active one is that of a man who worked in the pub and who killed his wife and her lover in the 1682. He was contacted during a séance and admitted what he had done before hanging himself from a beam. He said his name was Rex Bocon and also admitted stealing treasure from a parish church, where his father was vicar, and hiding it at the inn. He appears on frequent occasion with a most unhappy, and mournful,

Angel Inn, Guildford

face. Another is the earthbound spirit of the highwayman, Tom Hardy. He used the pub as his headquarters before he went out on his violent crimes and was eventually caught and hanged. Following his execution he returned to the pub in spirit and is still seen in various parts of it, dressed in his criminal uniform. Many years ago these manifestations were investigated by Donald Page and Canon John Pearce-Higgins, well-known psychical research experts.

Surrey

Angel Inn, Guildford
An apparition of a soldier in a foreign-style uniform has been seen in the crypt between the Angel and a nearby shop. On one occasion he stayed long enough in a bedroom at the Angel for a person to make a sketch of him. There are also reports of ghosts and phantoms being seen in the thirteenth-century cellars of the hotel. These also included escape routes between the hotel and other town houses for those on the run during times of persecution. It is the oldest hostelry in Guildford. During the reign of Queen Elizabeth I it was decreed 9 p.m. was late enough for servants to be on licensed premises in the town or be punished by jail.

Barley Mow, Englefield Green
In 1859 a Frenchman was fatally wounded in the last duel in the country on a nearby hill. Frederic Cournet was carried to this village inn where he died. He was buried in Egham Churchyard but his ghost still haunts the Barley Mow. Glasses have been smashed and sounds of sword fighting in the night have been heard at this three-centuries-old pub. One guest, when it was a coaching inn, was the novelist, George Eliot.

Bell Inn, East Molesey

Bell Inn, East Molesey

A five-centuries-old inn known locally as the 'Crooked House' because it has twisted over the years. One of the first bridge crossings over the Thames was built near here from Hampton Court. Prior to that there were a large number of ferry boats to make the crossing. Among regular customers at the inn was the highwayman, Claude Duval, at the time of Charles II. He had been a footman to the Duke of Richmond before he got into bad company and fled to France where he turned high-class swindler. One of his con tricks was to persuade the confessor to the King of France he could turn base metal into gold. He was hanged at Tyburn in January 1670. Duval has been seen wandering in the myriad of small and beamed bars in a long cloak and tricorne hat.

Britannia, Richmond

In one of the delightful lanes of Richmond is the Britannia which was modelled on the Duchess of Richmond. Britannia was the Roman name for Britain. The first medal struck of Britannia as a symbol was in 1665 and the model was Frances Stewart, a mistress of Charles II. The name Britannia for ships has been used by the Royal Navy for over 400 years. There have been heard cries and moans from an upper floor and said to those from a servant girl who here died many years ago in suspicious circumstances. Others have reported seeing the girl in a bar wearing a sacking apron and mob cap on her head.

Crown Inn, Old Oxted

Severe chills and footsteps are experienced at this Surrey inn. A woman in a long dress has been seen on an upstairs landing. A previous landlord and his wife left parted on somewhat acrimonious terms in the 1930s and it is thought to be the landlady wandering about and still venting her spleen. It may be the inn is haunted by two women, as a servant girl called Emy killed herself there in the 1850s, and was contacted by a medium for a television programme.

Britannia, Richmond

George Inn, Chertsey

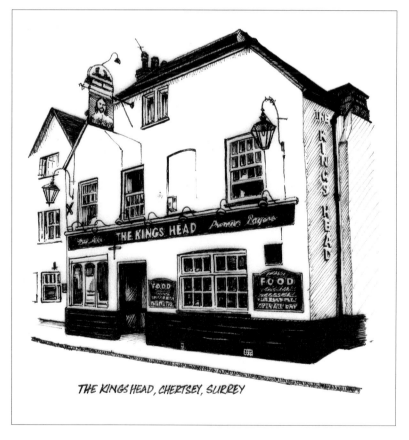

*King's Head,
Chertsey*

George Inn, Chertsey

A fine, old, coaching inn with two resident ghosts that have been seen over the years. One has been described as an aged monk with a cowl and the other a man in Victorian-style dress. This man has been seen in one bar as though waiting for somebody. He is described as a bit of a dandy and there is a strong smell of cigar smoke coming from him. There has also been much poltergeist activity, especially in the kitchen and the sound of a woman weeping in an upstairs room.

Greyhound, Carshalton

Built over 300 years ago it was a noted centre for cockfighting and other similar pursuits. For many years spare horses were kept at the Greyhound to help pull carts out of the mud when they got stuck. One morning a traveller in a long cloak was found dead on the doorstep having frozen to death during the night. His spirit still haunts the pub. Recently, when work was being done, a marble mosaic of a greyhound was found and thought to have been made by Italian artisans some 250 years ago.

Greyhound Inn, Lingfield

Over four-centuries-old, this pub is haunted by a boy of about seven seen wearing an Eton-style collar and jacket. The lad is said to have died in 1825 in sad circumstances and has been known to tug on the hem of women's skirts. There are some people described as 'sensitives' and one of these was tested by York University. He visited the pub in 1976 after being told that the pub, built in 1584, was haunted and made an investigation. The sensitive saw a small boy aged about eight wearing a grey suit with white collar. He reported a huge drop in temperature. Members of the kitchen staff complain about being touched by unseen hands, having parts of their bodies tweaked and kitchen equipment that keeps disappearing.

King's Arms Royal Hotel, Godalming

A right Royal Phantom may still lurk here three centuries after Peter the Great of Russia stayed at this inn. Such dreadful things did occur during their residence here that since then a poltergeist has haunted their rooms. From time to time glasses and other objects are hurled about in the rooms they used. Even more extraordinary was the tale of the woman of Godalming, one Mary Tofts who gave birth to rabbits in 1727. She claimed she had been made pregnant when frightened by a rabbit as she weeded in the garden. Tofts broke the news to the village people here at this inn and those credulous ones believed her.

King's Head, Chertsey

A barmaid at this town pub was rudely awakened when the bedclothes were stripped from her. Standing at the end of the bed was an elderly monk. There have been other sightings of the lubricous cleric at this sixteenth-century pub with a secret passage leading to a priest hole. During the War of the Roses a nephew of the Earl of Warwick was caught and condemned to die at Chertsey. When the bell tolled at St Peter's church it was the signal for his execution. But the bell did not ring, for his lover, Blanche Heriot, had made her way into the belfry and hung on to the clapper until his reprieve came through from the king. This gave rise to the American ballad, *Hang on the bell, Nelly, Hang on the bell.*

Marquis of Granby, Esher

Following the Battle of Warburg in the Seven Years War, John Manners, Marquis of Granby, ordered 300,000 pints of porter for the country to drink in honour of that occasion. He also gave pensions to his troops and many opened pubs with this money and, of course, called them the Marquis of Granby. This pub is mentioned in Dickens's *Pickwick Papers* when Sam Weller goes to visit his mother who worked there as a cook. At the top of the house is a cupboard that no one has dared to open in many a long year. Dogs, cats, children and other sensitive souls keep well away from it. For some years a bible was kept propped up against the door to keep it closed against some evil thing. Even so there have been many reports over the years of a darkly clad woman walking about in the night and her dress swishes in the dark. As soon as she is spotted she disappears into the nearest wall.

Queen's Head, Weybridge

An elderly woman apparition and two gentlemen appear here on a regular basis at this 300-year-old former coaching inn. She is known as 'The Lady' and is seen wearing a pleated skirt with a pinafore and has grey waved hair. When she appears there is a blue tinge around her according to the people who have seen her. The two men, wearing grey trousers and hobnailed boots, have been seen walking together and talking to each other through the bar. Glasses have been moved about and tonic bottles exploded while hand driers suddenly turn on in the middle of the night. From time to time a baby is heard crying from an empty room.

Roebuck, Richmond

A well known hostelry on Richmond Hill with its famous view of the bend in the river Thames across the sloping meadows, is home to a medium-height man who appears as a white mist. He floats across a room to disappear near a window and then seen making his way towards the river. There have also been reports of falling temperatures as he wanders in the pre-dawn.

White Hart, Wood Street

An old village pub near the green with two resident indwells. One is a man who has been seen to walk in, go up to the bar and then disappear. On one occasion a previous landlord known as Old Tom, saw him come in after closing time. The landlord was talking to a barman at the time and said, 'Tell him to bugger off, we are closed'. But no one was there. A female ghost has been seen checking the cutlery layouts and on several occasions the whole setting has been turned around. Some years ago a large knife hanging in the kitchen suddenly started swinging back and forth. But when the landlord went to touch it the knife stopped immediately. As the licensee said on my visit there, 'It seems they come back every time there is a new landlord – just to make sure they are running it properly'. In the 300-year-old fireplace there is a hook for smoking hams.

Sussex

Angel, Petworth

A five-centuries-old inn at one of the county's most attractive towns. At one time there was just a hole in the ceiling to allow smoke to rise from the inglenook fireplace which is still extant. An elderly woman, who was waiting for a friend, saw her crash down the stairs to her doom and was so shocked she died herself within a couple of days. Every now and again she is seen sitting at the inglenook in old-fashioned garb.

Bat & Ball, Ditchling Road, Brighton

The resident ghost here is thought to be that of a former landlady. A recent landlady was in the bar one night cashing up and saw at the end of the bar a barefooted woman wearing a white nightdress that came down to just below the knee. This woman started to dance round and round the bar and then when she got to the corner of the bar, just disappeared out into the street. An elderly customer told her that there had been a former landlady, most extrovert, who used to dance through the bar. One barman, after closing time, saw a middle-aged woman with grey hair, grey blouse and black skirt with a belt walking through. He thought she had been locked in the toilets at closing time and called out to her. She ignored him and three steps later she just disappeared.

Bath Arms, Meeting House Lane, Brighton
Originally this town-centre pub was called the True Briton when it was built in 1863. Three years later it changed its name to the Bath Arms to reflect the fashionable baths then being opened in the town. An early landlord committed suicide by walking into the waves on the front and then swimming out to sea. He has been reported over the years appearing back at the Bath Arms in wet clothing. There have been sightings in the pub of a man wearing a tricorne hat and old-fashioned clothing walking through the bar ignoring all the customers. A barmaid cleaning up after midnight saw a middle-aged man leaning against a pillar dressed in a black Victorian coat and a black hat. Staff and customers have witnessed glasses suddenly flying off the shelf to smash on the floor while bottles have moved along shelves when no one has been near to them.

Bell Inn, Iden
Almost 1,000 years old, it was there at the time of the Norman Conquest and was run by monks for pilgrims. There are two ghosts here. One has been seen in the gentlemen's lavatory and to walk out through a wall. At one time there had been a door at this point. The second, a middle-aged man, has been seen in the dining area near the fireplace. A pre-occupation with trees shows in the village history as, in 1586, John Brown was given permission to cut down an elm tree in the grounds of the Bell. In 1613 Robert Chandler was taken to court for carrying off an ash tree bough blown down in a storm and in 1642 John Young was arrested for felling an oak without a licence.

Blackboys, Blackboys
A picturesque inn with a huge lily pond and a spreading chestnut tree, it is named after Richard Blackboys, owner of the local estate in the fourteenth-century. During the night there have been footsteps and a drop in temperature. It is said to be Annie Starr, an eighteenth-century maid, and daughter of the landlord, who was made pregnant and then abandoned. She is said to be looking for the man who betrayed her and the baby who died shortly afterwards.

Black Lion, Black Lion Street, Brighton
This town pub was built as a brewery in 1546 by Deryck Carver, a Flemish immigrant. They used to hold anti-Catholic meetings here and eventually Carver was caught and became the first Protestant martyr when he was burned in a barrel at Lewes in 1555. The Black Lion Brewery closed in 1968 and the present Black Lion was built in 1974 using much of the original cobbles and slates and the sixteenth-century cellars still remain. One barman, working in the cellars, saw a number of beer crates being moved around the cellar as though being pushed by someone. On other occasions reserve gas cylinders, that had been left tied to a wall with straps, were scattered across the floor but the straps were still locked in place. A building worker on renovation awoke one night in his room to see a figure lit up by the street lights outside the pub walk around his room before disappearing.

Blackboys, Blackboys

Bow Street Runner, Hove

Blue Anchor, Portslade

Over the years there have been sightings of a little old lady wearing a grey dress. There is no story of who she is but, from time to time, beer taps have just turned off as well as gas cylinders bringing the beer from the cellars. One previous landlord was outside the pub moving crates of beer bottles when he heard a woman's voice say 'Door, door'. The door was closing on him and, had he not caught it in time, he would have been locked out as it had a self-locking device and there was no one else in the pub at the time to let him back in.

Bow Street Runner, Hove

In the middle of a terrace of houses this pub was built on the site of the first police station at Hove and named after the first police officers in uniform. In 1830 the police officers wore a black tailcoat with a red collar, white trousers and a black top hat. One night a prostitute and her pimp were arrested for being drunk and disorderly and put into the cells. She died there and since then an apparition in Victorian dress has appeared through the rear walls of the pub from where the cells once stood and into the bar. She has been seen by several customers sitting in the bar and there have been knocking sounds from the rear wall as though someone is trying to get out. Metal caps have come off beer bottles but the beer remains inside the bottle although large measures have disappeared from the gin bottle. There was a picture at the pub of a man with a very thin face but occasionally the features would alter. This picture disappeared in 1985 and no one knows its whereabouts. Bottles have been known to fly across the bar and one securely fixed curtain on a brass rail fell away from the wall.

Brunswick, Holland Road, Hove

A couple moved in as managers of this near seaside pub and discovered a large quantity of bric-a-brac in the cellars. The woman found a framed picture and when she cleaned the glass found it was not a painting but a famed certificate for a poetry competition and with the name, George Bennett. At this point the temperature dropped several degrees and she saw a man move across the barrels and floor before he suddenly disappeared. An elderly male customer told her that the pub was haunted by an old poet and the story was that if one moves the certificate it disturbs the soul of the dead poet. Other managers have reported lights going on and off with bumps and bangs. Late one night a barman looked up and saw a man with grey hair wearing blue trousers and a grey pullover who walked into a wall and disappeared.

Bull Hotel, Ditchling

Almost 700 years ago a market was set up at Ditchling under a charter from Edward II. It is not clear how long afterwards the Bull Hotel was built but it was existence in 1636 when it was listed in *A Catalogue of Taverns in Tenne Shires about London*. Local historians place it further back by about 120 years. Bar staff there have regularly seen a full pint slowly slide along a bar and crash onto the ground although no person was nearby. Shortly after these curious incidents there is a rattling of the door handle as though someone were leaving. There are also reports of interior doors opening and closing although sometimes ★they have even been locked. Paintings on the wall of the pub's upper floor have been moved about during the night. Even more strange there have been reports that beds that had been made up adopting a slight bump in the middle as though a cat were underneath. But when the duvet or cover is pulled back there is nothing there, although the spot is warm to touch.

Cat Inn, West Hoathly

On the run from pursuers after a vicious murder a man turned up here for refuge. Built in 1450 it was a haunt of smugglers and the man, Jacob Hirsch (or sometimes Harris) thought he would be safe here. Then he noticed that the landlady, Mary Brooks, was watching him and realised he had blood all over his sleeve and made off again. This time he hid up a chimney in a nearby manor house but some local militia men turned up and started a fire. Hirsch collapsed in the smoke and fell down onto the flames and was arrested. Later that year Hirsch was indicted for murder and hanged and then his body cut up and taken to Wivelsfield where it was strung up in a gibbet and left there. After this it became known as Jacob's Post and people would travel miles to cut small slivers of wood from it that were supposed to be curative. His ghost turns up at the Cat Inn from time to time when a man with wide-staring eyes is seen in the bar and what appears to be blood on his old-fashioned jacket.

Cock Inn, Wivelsfield Green

Once known as the Fighting Cock when there was a cockpit nearby, it was used by smugglers as a halfway house between London and Brighton. Since the 1940s there have been stories of objects being thrown around rooms with tremendous force. There are also cold areas. Curtains have come away from their rings to lie on the floor in crumpled heaps. One landlord woke up when he heard a window screech as it opened during the night. Investigating he found the window had locks on it but was wide open. Trying to close it he found it had been forced open so violently he could not do so. Another manager awoke to see the apparition of a woman, dressed in white, cross his room and disappear through a wall. She has been spotted in the bar as she walks across and, again, disappears through a solid wall.

Above left: *Colonnade Bar, New Road, Brighton*

Above right: *Crown & Anchor, Shoreham*

Colonnade Bar, New Road, Brighton

Next door to the Theatre Royal is this superb Edwardian-style bar in red plush, mirrors and photographs of actors who have appeared over the years. Once the ladies of the night paraded underneath the arches of this Georgian building. The theatre was opened in 1822 and was regularly visited by the Victorian Prince of Wales and is haunted by a Grey Lady. She has been described by many staff and actors who have seen her as about 5ft 6ins tall, between fifty and sixty-years-old and of a commanding presence. (Danny la Rue insisted she had been trying on his wigs whilst he was out). The bar is haunted by another Grey Lady who sits in a corner. One manager said:

> She was wearing a lovely, grey, chiffon dress. She was no way frightening, but, before I could say anything, with a sweet smile she disappeared. The odd thing was she did not seem to have any feet or ankles.

Cricketers, Black Lion Lane, Brighton

This is probably the oldest pub in Brighton said to have been built in 1545. Originally it was called the Last and Fish Cart; a last was a total of 10,000 fish, but the pub was generally referred to as 'the Last'. This became the Cricketers when it was taken over by a Mr Jutten who played for Brighton Cricket Club. Next door was the original animal pound last used in 1887 when a drunk shepherd or drover was arrested for being unable to care for his flock. Among famous luminaries to have used this hostelry were Graham Green and even Jack the Ripper. There are some who maintain that the real Jack was a man called Roslyn D'Onston a Sussex journalist and ex-army surgeon who was into black magic. Over the years there have been several ghostly happenings. One manager reported beer barrels being rolled about in the night but when she investigated nothing was out of place. Bottles and glasses have jumped from shelves and several times footsteps were heard on stairs when no one was about. A man in charge of the restaurant tells of an eerie experience when he went round after closing time blowing out all the table candles. Several minutes later he returned to the restaurant to find them all alight again. Many times a man dressed in a long, black coat with a wide, brimmed, black hat and very pale features has been seen going up the stairs. A woman customer, who went to the ladies' lavatory in the dark, felt two hands grip her around the head and stroke her forehead.

Crown & Anchor, Shoreham

Once a wooden figurehead of St George decorated the front of the nearby Royal George and given to Eric Wardroper of the Crown & Anchor when the Royal George closed. This crashed down in the 1920s and was replaced by a wooden figurehead of a pirate-bold standing on the prow of a boat. A French girl, brought ashore by a soldier/sailor after the Napoleonic Wars, was then abandoned when she became pregnant. She worked here as a serving wench and then committed suicide by throwing herself from a rear window; she still haunts the pub. Those who have seen her describe as being pale faced, dressed in grey material and muttering in what sounds like the French language.

Dr Brightons, King's Road, Brighton

A superb name for this pub that was previously known as the Star & Garter Hotel. In the 1920s the landlord changed the name after reading William Makepeace Thackeray's *The Newcomes*. Thackeray said in this book, 'One of the best physicians is kind, cheerful, merry Doctor Brighton'. One maid tells of a time when she was in her room with a friend. The floor started to shake and vibrate and all the ornaments and cosmetics on a table were blown away and then a mirror cracked from side to side. Then they saw an old man sitting in an armchair in the corner of the room. One barman went to the lavatory and, while in there, he was suddenly tapped on each shoulder by a strong hand but no one was there. Other guests have said they have seen the shadowy figure of a man appear in the mirrors in the same toilets. A window cleaner told one manager that he kept finding fingerprints on certain windows. They were checked and found to be those of a small child although no children were allowed in that part of the inn. It is thought that these fingerprints came from a young boy who was in the cellars with his mother and suddenly crashed his head against a beer barrel with fatal results.

Druid's Head, Brighton Place, Brighton

Over 500-years-old, the building was a private house before it became pub in 1830. It was called the Druids Head after a ring of stones, thought to be associated with the druids, was found nearby. There were two tunnels from the pub; one leading to the sea for the smugglers and the other to the Royal Pavilion that is said to have been used by the Prince Regent to buy stocks of brandy and for assignations with his women friends. There are said to be three ghosts here, one a man who died in one of the tunnels and two children. There have been poltergeist activities with bottles and glasses whizzing around and mirrors suddenly misting over. Lights go on and off, and, when checked, the switches were found to be in good order. Apart from the middle-aged man in workman's clothing seen from time to time and the two children dressed in Victorian-style clothing, a ghostly woman has been seen in the bar. One Sunday lunch time a barmaid saw a woman dressed in red waiting to be served. She spoke to her but the woman just disappeared in front of her.

Dr Brightons, King's Road, Brighton

Dyke Tavern, Dyke Road, Brighton

They call her the Grey Lady at this out-of-town pub that was once called the Windmill Inn. A woman working here was cleaning the beer pump handles when she felt as though she was being watched. She turned around and, near the fireplace about 3yds away, she saw a woman dressed a full-length grey dress with a high collar and pleats on the front. Although she looked solid her face was very grey the witness reported and then she just dissolved away. The Grey Lady has been seen on many occasions by other members of the staff who have spoken to her only to see her disappear. There have been odd poltergeist activities over the years with objects moving about and beer supplies being cut off from the cellar. Curious footsteps have been heard outside the bathroom but no one could be seen. The inn sign is a fascinating one, depicting the Devil with horns in the full moon.

George & Dragon, Dragons Green

Almost everyone's dream of what a country pubs should look like, small and beamed with a splendid red-tiled roof. At this pub is the gravestone where the son of a former landlord is buried in the garden. The main bar is haunted by two old farmers dressed in Victorian-style clothing with either gaiters or sackcloth leggings. It is also here where the annual dwile-flonking takes place. This is a game for twelve people dressed in old fashioned rural gear and a beer-soaked cloth, a dwile, at the end of a pole which is thrown at one of the players when the music stops. (Well, that seems to be the rules).

Golden Cannon, St George's Road, Brighton

The pub is said to be haunted by a previous landlord who hanged himself in the cellars in about 1800. One previous landlady said they called him Frank. She said that on occasion Frank comes out and taps you on the shoulder for a laugh. When a later landlady's husband died in the 1980s he warned her that if he saw she was drinking too much he would come back to haunt her and tip her glass over. Several times, over the years since then, her glass would suddenly turn itself upside down, she said recently.

Golden Lion, Manchester Street, Brighton

The ghost here is said to be a former landlady who died in the Golden Lion and had a hatred of plastic flowers. One cleaner was working in the basement and saw some plastic plants actually leap from the pots and she heard an angry woman's voice shouting at her. On several occasions crates and bottles were moved about from their proper positions in the cellars. A technical man from a brewery called and while he was standing in the cellar was struck on the back of the head with some object. During a search they found a piece of metal made of heavy grey metal which seemed to be from a small statue and carried the face of the Devil himself with horns. Two women working at the pub were leaving when they were struck on the back of their heads with wet teabags although no one was about. One of these women reports seeing a previous landlady, whom she knew, who had died quite young, suddenly appear in the basement bar and then disappear without saying a word.

Greyhound, East Street, Brighton

For years this town-centre pub has been pestered by a mischievous imp with a penchant for electronic equipment, especially the video player. People would be watching a film when suddenly the video would stop and then go into fast mode. On occasions it even threw the tape back out of the machine and onto the floor. One even more alarming trick was to suddenly stop and the tape would move in and out of the recorder. There has also been trouble with the beer lines to the cellar. Over the years there have been two apparitions seen; a tall woman dressed in white in her early twenties and a small child.

Hangleton Manor, Hangleton Lane, Hove

A dovecote in the grounds is said to have been cursed by a monk who hated the bird droppings from it. There have been stories of the tramping of boots in the long gallery and the sounds of heavy balls being rolled in what was an Elizabethan skittle alley. One tenant saw a man dressed in white enter a room with the sound of spurs from his feet as he crossed the room only to disappear. There are said to be two women ghosts here, one of whom pushes at people, and said to be the ghost of a servant girl who was killed when she fell downstairs. Another is also a servant girl who was seduced by her employer and became pregnant. When the baby was born she threw the child out of the attic window and started screaming. Her screams can still be heard and, on occasion, a pair of white hands suddenly appears in a corridor. They have also been seen resting on a bedroom door handle. As well as the hands becoming visible there has also been seen the lower half of a body in a brown, silky skirt, running through the house with a strange rustling sound. A group of employees were waiting for a taxi one night when suddenly they saw the toilet door burst open and the main door suddenly unlatch and open up as though someone had just burst through to the outside.

George & Dragon,
Dragon's Green

John's Cross Inn, John's Cross, near Robertsbridge

Horse and Groom, Islingwood Road, Brighton

A rather happy customer of this pub many years ago used to have a favourite seat against a bar window. After his death he would turn up and be seen sitting behind a pint of beer. He was known to all and sundry as 'Fred'. A former cleaner at the pub saw him sitting there one day and shouted at him, 'Be on your way Fred. There is no place for you here,' and he disappeared before her eyes. On one occasion three men were sitting at the table when a pint glass on the window shelf behind Fred's favourite seat began to move. It slowly moved along about 3ft and leapt from the shelf to the floor where it smashed. The landlord of the time was intrigued by this and even tested the shelf with a spirit level and found it to be exactly level. Fred has even been up to his larks in the cellar and gas cylinders turn off and he has fun with the glass washing machine. Several times this has been switched off and then turned itself on to rattle noisily for three minutes.

John's Cross Inn, John's Cross, near Robertsbridge

An ancient roadside inn where strange things have occurred. On one occasion six Perrier bottles in a locked room came out of a sealed packet and lined themselves up on the bar. Barrels in the cellar and furniture in the bar have moved about and ashtrays have suddenly tipped up along the bar. Over the years there have been reports of a bent and elderly woman standing outside the front door with a bag over her shoulders. When anyone has spoken to her she has looked round and then disappeared. In what they call the smallest restaurant in the county, it has only four places, there appears to be ghost figure on the wall. This is the handiwork of the landlord, Bob Russell, a noted inn-sign painter, and is a splendid example of his *trompe d'oeil* work.

Lion, St James Street, Brighton

There have been several tragic incidents here over the years and may well have given rise to the frequent hauntings. In 1936, the then licensee, Henry Metcalfe, shot his wife and killed her with three shots to the body. Then he shot himself and was found lying dead beside her. Some years later a maid working here was found dead in the staff quarters and appeared to have died from shock. A medical examiner said that she had a look of absolute terror on her face but was, otherwise, in good health. Since those incidents there have been times when doors would open or close on their own and there would be sound of bracelets jangling and the odour of a strong perfume. Another landlady resting before the fire shortly before opening time heard sounds behind her and, to her amazement, saw the bar stools being moved as though people were sitting down at the bar for a drink. While retiring in her sitting room another landlady felt someone grip her shoulder and, when she looked up, there was someone or something standing there wearing grey.

Marlborough, Princes Street, Brighton

A genuine Victorian drama took place at this pub at the turn of the nineteenth century when a landlord brutally killed his wife during a row. He struck her with a bottle and was charged with murder but this was later reduced to manslaughter. Since 1900 there have been weird incidents associated with the unfortunate woman, Mrs Packham. Gas cylinders have turned themselves off and bottles have leapt off shelves. Keys used to operate the cash tills refuse to operate but work perfectly well minutes later. Several times the misty shape of a woman has been seen in the main bar. One assistant manager heard the rattles of chains on one occasion. She investigated to find chains in the room that had been used years ago for lifting barrels, but no one was near or had been for some time.

Mermaid Inn, Rye

Two ghosts have been seen at this inn fighting a duel with swords. Dressed in sixteenth-century clothing one has been seen to stab the other and drag his corpse across the room. One of the oldest pubs in the country it was rebuilt in 1420 and has a background of smuggling and other dreadful incidents. In the local town hall is kept a cage containing the head of Butcher Breads who attempted to murder a local mayor and magistrate at the inn. Instead he stabbed the man's brother-in-law who had been wearing the mayoral garments. Breads was hanged in 1743 and the skull kept at the town hall. Turn away from this if you are squeamish. The rest of him was boiled up as a soup for medicine. Another local ghost is that of a monk who eloped with a local girl. They were caught and walled up to die. His magnificent singing voice was turned into a turkey gobble as a further punishment. He is still with us in Turkey Cock Lane, Rye.

New Inn, Hurstpierpoint

A rather exotic phantom has taken up residence here and leaves the aroma of a good cigar in the cellars. But whoever it is can be a bit naughty at times and glasses and bottles have leaped from shelves and on one occasion a leather strip of horses brasses came away from a hook and landed several feet away on a table. A former landlord was out in the garden and heard a large explosion and rushed in to find an ashtray had broken into eight exact triangles of glass. This happened again two weeks later, but without any explanation. A local couple in the pub were astounded to see a light bulb drop from its fixture onto the ground but it kept alight all the way down until it smashed. A drayman working at the pub told of a man he saw walk through the cellars and then disappear into a wall.

Old Ship, Ship Street, Brighton

A most impressive hotel once owned by Nicholas Tettersell who, as a ship's captain, helped Charles II escape to France in October 1651. He owned a coal brig called the *Surprise* and, when the king was reinstated, Tettersell renamed it the *Royal Escape* and made sure King Charles knew about it. Tettersell was appointed captain in the Royal Navy on full pay and pension. With this he bought the Olde Shippe as it was then in 1671. Some years later he was appointed the High Constable of Brighton. The first record of this inn is 1665 but it is known that there was another inn on the site in 1559. Among guests at the Old Shippe for society balls was the Prince Regent. It has had a reputation for being haunted for many years. On one occasion a chambermaid went into a room in the oldest part and saw a man and woman sitting on the bed. As she was explaining what she was doing the couple disappeared from view. Night porters have seen grey shapes appear and disappear in the ballroom. On one occasion two night porters witnessed a shape at the bottom of the stairs that turned into a small child crying and wearing old-fashioned clothing. Again, this disappeared as they watched it.

Plough Inn, Pycombe

Because of the number of fatal accidents on the main road that passes through the area, a morgue was set up in the Plough cellar in the early 1930s. There have been good reports of several apparitions being seen over the years and one of them is a nun in a grey habit. Glasses and bottles have come off shelves without good reason and, even on windless nights in the summertime, curtains have suddenly been ripped down with such force the rails and fixings have come down too. Several customers have told the landlords that when they have been to the ladies' lavatory they have come to face to face with a nun. Another customer who was being served saw a woman in a black dress and white pinafore behind the landlady but she gradually disappeared.

Mermaid Inn, Rye

Ram Inn, West Firle

Queen's Head, Icklesham

An old man has been seen sitting by a fireplace at this inn. He is dressed as a shepherd, or farm worker, in an old pull-down hat and he is chewing straw. It is said to be Mr Gutsell, a former landlord, who died there in the nineteenth century. Built in 1632 and converted into an ale house in the early 1830s, the Queen's Head is a timber-framed building with the name on the roof that can be seen from many miles away. The fine tessellated inn sign on the wall shows the late Queen Mother as Warden of the Cinque Ports.

Ram Inn, West Firle

A ram has appeared on the sign of Worshipful Company of Clothworkers since the fourteenth century, and as a pub name in sheep-breeding areas or where wool business is conducted. This Ram is a five-centuries-old former coaching inn once used as a courthouse for local criminals. It is haunted by a young girl who was a basket maker and who was found dead in an attic. She had been living rough and had a deformed leg and the landlord took her in. Now there are sounds of her limping up a narrow stairway to the room where she died. The pub name is also part of the heraldry of Sir John Gage, vice-chancellor to Henry VIII, whose family introduced the greengage to England.

Regency Tavern, Russell Square, Brighton

Over 130 years ago two upper-class lodging houses stood on this site catering for long-stay visitors to Brighton. When it became the Regency Tavern the site was extended through to an old bootmaker's shop that had been founded in 1893. One of the ghosts that haunts this inn is a disabled girl, the daughter of a boot maker named William Moore. She died, after believing that she smelled gas in her room and jumped from the first floor window. She told this to her father as she lay dying in hospital. When she does appear it is usually on the first floor of the Regency and she is quite clearly disabled and with a very pale face. A former landlady, Mrs Edlin, has also taken up residence here after a long spell as licensee at the inn. She, too, has been seen on the first floor wearing late-Victorian clothing. One barman reported articles being moved about in his room after it had been locked up and no one had gone in. Occasionally, in the bar, chairs that have been placed on top of tables at closing time were found to be back on the floor by morning time. A part-time barman at the Regency was working in the cellars transferring a beer line when he felt he was being watched. He turned and saw a woman some distance from him. But she was surrounded by a green haze and with a most malevolent face. He said she was wearing a long dress with a high collar. He fell down behind a barrel and then, he says, he felt her pass right through him, and described the sensation as though it were sharp fingers of ice penetrating him.

Royal Oak, East Lavant

Two smugglers murdered a Revenue man at this pub 200 years ago during a gun fight. They were tried for their wickedness and eventually dispatched to meet their maker; one of them, however, never made it. Well, all right, one cannot vouch for the other one either. Since that date a tall, thin and bearded man has been seen wandering around the pub but mainly in the bedrooms. Three miles north of Chichester it is an old coaching inn with an old grandfather clock. The eldest son of a previous landlord tinkered with this clock and later the boys were visited by things in the night and the clock chimed at uneven times. They said they saw a small man with a very full beard, and old-fashioned clothing coming out of their room and smiling at them.

Royal Oak, Poynings

More than quaint it is an exotic ghost at this timbered village pub. A former landlord here was a flamboyant fellow given to wearing tartan tunics. By this uniform he is still known as he appears from time to time walking through the bar and into the kitchen. Several times staff have spotted him sitting at a kitchen table and also at a table in the dining area. On other occasions he has walked through the bar to where a trapdoor to the cellar once existed, and disappears down there. A barman said that the apparition actually looked at him and gave a civil nod as he went past. One couple who took over the pub, report being awakened at 3 a.m. to hear sounds of a merry party going on in the bar with conversation and glasses clinking. When they went down the bar was empty.

Royal Oak, Wivelsfield

A brick-and-tile-hung roadside inn, it was once called Jacob's Cross after a felon executed for murder. Jacob Hirsch, a travelling peddler murdered two people and tried to kill the landlord, Richard Miles, and then escaped to East Hoathly. Many years ago a woman and her daughter heard excited sounds coming from one part of the room. Looking at a wall mirror they saw a large religious cross had appeared on it. It was dark grey, slightly misty, and remained for some time before disappearing. A manager awoke at 4 a.m. and saw a woman in a long white dress, grey shawl and old-fashioned hair net. She was pushing at what had been a door many years ago, but since bricked up, and then disappeared through it.

Schooner, Shoreham

Smugglers used a secret tunnel down to the nearby waterfront and beach from this inn. Many years ago a little girl and her nanny were drowned in these cellars when they were cut off by a rising tide. A former licensee woke up to find her hair being stroked and a woman has been seen walking in the cellars with a child. Two mediums were called in to investigate the phenomenon and one of them fell down in a swoon and started speaking like a child. A bar manager saw a strange white light about 3ft across. He described the outer edge as electric blue and then saw a small red haired child aged six on the floor with her hands at her face.

Seven Stars, Robertsbridge

A pub has stood here for about 500 years and near to a former Cistercian monastery. The seven stars was a well known sign in the Middle Ages and referred to the celestial crown of the Virgin Mary. Over the years at this inn there have been sightings of the ghostly Red Monk in his earthly perambulations. In the rear bar is a wall mural of William, Lord Abbot of the abbey from 1192 to 1219 and it is thought to be he who is the Red Monk. Wearing a cowl he carries two seals; on the left is the Common Seal and on the right, the Counter Seal. It is surrounded by a fine wall cover with Latin words woven into it. Local history has it that the original building may go back to the time of Richard I. Horace Walpole stayed here in the mid-1750s and was surprised to find it the haunt of smugglers, highwaymen, prostitutes and other ne'er-do-wells. In the nearby church of St Mary the Virgin is the grave of Peter Sparkes who died in 1683 and said to be 127 years old.

Shades, Crawley

The Shades opened in the fourteenth century and later there were holding cells with an underground passageway to the George Hotel. Condemned prisoners were led through to be hanged on the wooden structure on the market square which is still there. Shades is an old-fashioned word for ghosts and this pub is haunted by a pipe-smoking man who uses the ladies' lavatory and a woman in grey with a small child. One man went to his room to find the bed on fire that could never be explained. It was the same room where the woman and child appear. Landladies have experienced the front door bell ringing at 6 a.m. to find no one there and the bell jammed.

Shelley's Bar, High Street, Lewes

A Queen's Counsel prosecuting at a local quarter sessions was lifted several inches from his bed during the night while staying at this inn. It was the scene of a suicide many years ago and poltergeists are still active. They say that one gentleman who had stayed in room No 26 in the 1930s left the room so quickly he left all his clothes behind and went and gassed himself in a nearby house belonging to a relation. The ghost of a Cavalier has been seen on the staircase in the sixteenth-century part of the hotel. On other occasions an old lady in a blue and white dress has been seen by guests and staff. It is named after the poet, Percy Bysshe Shelley, whose aunt once owned the place.

Shepherd & Dog, Fulking

An absolute treasure of a pub, it was once used by sheep drovers going to local sheep fairs and markets. It nestles below the South Downs and was built over 600 years ago. Inside the pub bucolic ephemera, including shepherds' crooks, abound. Every area in the country had their own way of counting sheep and in Sussex shepherds counted the sheep in pairs: wuntherum, twotherum, cockerum, cutherum, sheterum, shaterum, wineberrry, wigtail, tarry-diddle, den, with each word counting two sheep. The upstairs of the pub is haunted by a former landlord, Mr Liquorice, and downstairs by noisy poltergeists.

Seven Stars, Robertsbridge

Above: *Shepherd & Dog, Fulking*

Left: *Spread Eagle, Midhurst*

Six Bells, Chiddingley

An eighteenth-century hostelry opposite the village church, it has a large garden and fish pond. Here are many artifacts including a pianola with rolls of music, stuffed animals, prints and old political cartoons. A huge inglenook fireplace has a seat at each end and there are high-backed settles throughout. The pub garden is haunted by a big grey cat seen by people driving into the car park. A local wife, who poisoned her husband with an onion pie, was the last woman to be hanged publicly in 1856 at Lewes and she has been seen in one bar of the Six Bells holding a mixing bowl.

Spread Eagle, Midhurst

The American emblem is the white or bald-headed eagle but it goes back further than American history. It was used by the Romans and was marched at the head of their legions. This inn takes the emblem from a local family that bears it on their coat of arms. One part of the inn dates from about 1430 with half timbering and lattice windows and was used as a hunting lodge. In the main bedroom is a wig- powdering room used by travellers over the years and bears the date 1430 on the narrow black door. It is near to, and in this wig-powdering room, that the ghost of an elderly man with a bald head has been seen. Several witnesses have described him as wearing a judge's dress of scarlet robe, fur facings, black cravat and waistband and a scarlet hood. This description fits that of a high-court judge.

Stag, Hastings

There is a fascinating collection of mummified cats at this old smugglers inn and there is an old sea captain said to be still in residence who is often seen sitting in the bar. It also has its own game of Loggitts. During the nineteenth century efforts were made to build a new harbour at Hastings but this was broken up by the sea. In 1201 King John proclaimed British sovereignty of the seas from Hastings. There is still a maze of caves that had been used by smugglers. On occasions an organ has been heard being played from a nearby church when no one was there. The ghost of Thomas à Becket, the murdered archbishop has been seen in the town. There have also been reports of cries and groans and clinking of chains from dungeons built for prisoners. On certain bright days a mirage of Hastings Castle can be seen out at sea as it would have appeared centuries ago.

Stag's Head, Portslade

An interesting pub with a flint façade that contains a bust of the ghost that haunts the place. The pub dates back to about 1674 and the ghost has been seen on many occasions, usually in the cellar. Those who had spotted him, a man who was a potman many years ago, described him to an art student who built a bust of him that now rests on the bar. The ghostly potman has a quirky sense of humour and occasionally changes over the beer lines from full barrels to empty ones.

Star, Alfriston

This was once a hospice for pilgrims on their way to Canterbury. The red lion that takes pride of place outside the inn came off a Dutch naval ship at Sole Bay in 1672. Two ghosts have been seen here; one is described as dressed in medieval court wear and the other dressed a farmer of many years ago. He has been seen from time to time sitting in the lounge beneath the wall clock. One landlord was awakened one night to see the old farmer walk across his bedroom and peer at something on the wall before turning around and walking back. He described him as about sixty and wearing a floppy hat, an old-fashioned smock with pleats in it and leggings that had been tied with string and seemed to be made of a rough sackcloth. There have also been reports of people being locked in their rooms and having to use the internal telephone to be released.

Stag, Hastings

Stag's Head, Portslade

Union Inn, East Street, Rye

The Union is a reference to a political or important marriage union. Built on a hill and almost next door to Rye Museum, it is haunted by the unhappy soul of an unmarried mother who worked there and fell downstairs many years ago, breaking her neck. The other haunting is by a soldier in old-fashioned uniform seen sitting in a bar. In a glass-fronted space in a wall, some bones of a child were found and may have been connected with the unhappy mother above.

War-Bill-In-Tu, Warbleton

A bill was the word for several different kinds of sword-like weapons and this is a play on words on the inn name and the village name. Opposite the parish church the original inn was of the thirteenth century. However it is first recorded as having an innkeeper in 1642 at the outbreak of the English Civil War when Tasmania was discovered. Then it was described as the Two Tuns. Once built of two-storey brick and tile, it was rebuilt in 1969. It is haunted by Richard Woodman, a Sussex iron founder, who was burned at the stake at Lewes as a heretic. Woodman had called his rector 'Mr Facing-both-ways' for being a protestant under Henry VIII and a catholic under Queen Mary. Woodman took refuge at this inn before he was captured.

White Hart, High Street, Lewes

An important coaching inn since 1717 when John Law founded the Louisiana Company and the first Masonic lodge opened in London. Tom Paine started his Age of Reason and described his discussions at the White Hart as 'the cradle of American Independence'. The room where he held his discussions is now the Tudor or Sheriff's Room and is used by that official for the Lewes Crown Court. It has a copy of the American Constitution on the wall. It is here that several men have been sitting in a circle wearing very old-fashioned black clothing and hats. They always look up when seen and then suddenly disappear. In the mid-1550s some seventeen men and women were burned at the stake in Lewes by judges who were trying to impose the authority of the Pope. Before execution the martyrs were kept in the medieval wine cellars of this inn. It is thought that these are the ghosts that haunt the Tudor room. A previous landlord, William Verral, wrote the *Compleat System of Cookerie*.

White Horse, Ditchling

A male ghost with a propensity for stroking the heads of women has been in residence here for many years. Historians and mediums believe that this is closely associated with an incident in 1806. Mr Harnott, a previous landlord, woke up when he heard someone breaking their way through a window. In the bar he saw two men, Robert Bignall, smuggler and killer and John Tingley, another local criminal. Bignall pulled out his pistol but Mr Harnott grabbed him and held him while Tingley made his escape. In the ensuing struggle Harnott was shot dead. Following his trial Robert Bignall was hanged with a multitude of 3,000 there to watch him swing. They say that the ghost here is that of Bignall who was also known as a ladies' man.

Ye Castle, Bramber

On a hill above this inn is the ruined Bramber Castle and this hostelry is named after it. Over 800 years ago the castle was owned by William de Breose. King John questioned his loyalty

White Hart, High Street, Lewes

Ye Castle, Bramber

and wanted his children as hostages. The de Breose wife and children fled to Ireland but were captured. Taken to Corfe Castle, Dorset, they starved to death. Lord de Breose is still remembered in Welsh folklore as the 'Ogre of Abergavenny' for his extreme cruelty. The ghosts of the de Breose children are still about in Bramber and usually around Christmas time outside this inn. They have been seen looking up at the castle on the hill above the village, their old home. They are known locally as the 'Bramber Babes' and are seen begging for food while arrayed in ragged clothing. Some stories maintain that when it is particularly cold they appear in the bar of the inn. They always disappear when spoken to.

Warwickshire

Castle Inn, Edgehill

A most eccentric pub it was built originally as a folly some 200 years ago to commemorate the Battle of Edgehill over a century previously. Occasionally a Cavalier officer is seen as he canters through the bar on his horse. There have been sightings of a phantom army fighting on the fields of Edgehill. Along with sights there have been reports of the sound of drums and the cries of the wounded and dying. There have even been visions in the sky of regiments of soldiers doing battle. Charles I who escaped, and his standard bearer Sir Edmund Verney, slain on the field of battle, were seen long after the conflict by two captains and a colonel who knew them well.

Sheaf and Sickle, Long Lawford

In years long gone corn was cut by sickle and gathered together in a sheaf. This would easily make an inn sign that could be understood by anyone at that time. When twelve clergymen, experienced in exorcism, were called in for a local job some stayed at this inn. One of them is said to have died in the pub and can still be seen from time to time in clerical garb. They had been called from all corners of the country to deal with a haunting at the nearby Lawford Hall. A one-armed man haunted that hall for years until the twelve were asked to exorcise the malevolent one. They claimed they had closed him into a bottle and thrown him into deep water, but to no avail; he was seen for years afterwards driving around in a coach- and-six outside this pub.

Haunch of Venison, Salisbury

Wiltshire

Haunch of Venison, Salisbury

Eccentric and delightful, in equal parts the pub was originally built as a church tower for the nearby St Thomas's church in 1320. An old woman in a white shawl appears from time to time to passers by and leaves behind a smell of freshly tilled earth. In 1903 a marked pack of cards and a mummified hand were found. Pubs named after game or the hunt are usually found near royal hunting grounds. Venison is usually thought to be just the flesh off deer but it derives from *venari*, Latin to hunt, and meant all types of prey. The expression to 'eat humble pie' is associated with this. The real word is umbles or numbles (fifteenth century) which was the offal and the skin flesh of the deer. This was the part that the poor people ate.

King & Queen, Highworth

A five-centuries-old inn with its own monk spirit and another phantom that goes through walls. In the nearby thirteenth-century church a 'robed ghost' has been seen and a figure in grey on the nearby street. A former landlord found his dogs bristling and howling with fright near a wall surrounding the pub. He looked up and saw a monk glide straight up and over the wall. This ghost has also been seen near the church and there is a passage between the pub and church. One landlord took out insurance of £100,000 against people being frightened by the ghosts. It is said the ghost here is a monk who broke chastity vows to have an affair with a local girl.

Red Lion, Avebury

Built on the site of a former monastery hospice it is said to be connected by a tunnel to nearby Longleat House, and has two ghosts. They have been seen as shapes, one black and the other white, both in separate rooms. There is also Florrie, a seventeenth-century ghost and a high priest of the Covenant of Earth Magic tried to exorcise her in 1997. This quite upset the then landlord, Pat McCann, and he told a local newspaper, 'This is my pub and he cannot go around exorcising spirits without my permission'. Some years ago another landlord put all his clocks forward an hour for BST and in the morning they had all been turned back again. The pub is not far from the stone circles with legend of untold forces. There are some 100 upright stones weighing as much as 60 tons each and inside that ring are the remains of two smaller circles. This is the only pub in the country inside a stone circle. When a television company was at the inn to make an episode of *Most Haunted*, a presenter, Yvette Fielding, felt the hand of someone behind her on her shoulder. This was said to have been Florence who has been haunting the place for thirty years. The television producer was also touched and scratched behind the neck and Florence made contact with four other members of the crew. Many years ago a man was murdered here and thrown down the well. That well is now glassed over but the spirit of the murdered man still roams the inn. Several of these ghosts have been identified by mediums.

Yorkshire

Black Bull, Haworth

It is uncertain when this inn was built but it was once a stopping place for coaches between Bradford and Colne in Lancashire. Over the years there have been strange happenings at the pub where Branwell Brontë was a regular customer. Residents have reported footsteps following them up and downstairs but nobody is there, cold hands stroking foreheads in the night and the sound of a child weeping although no families were staying at the time. One ghost has been described by some and closely resembles Branwell Brontë, with dishevelled red hair and a wild look in his eyes.

Black Swan, Peaseholme Green

The black swan was an original Roman joke by Juvenal who described it as a *rara avis*. The first time it appeared as an inn sign was in the sixteenth century and, perhaps, just referred the landlord's opinion of himself as a rare bird. This is the oldest pub in York going back over almost 600 years. There are two resident indwells here. One is a young woman with blonde hear who wears a long white dress and stares into the fireplace. She has been reported as glowing with colour. The second is a Victorian artisan wearing an old-fashioned bowler hat. He stands in the bar as though he is waiting for someone and then just disappears.

Busby Stoop, Carlton Miniott

In 1702 a man called Tom Busby was hanged on gallows and then gibbeted opposite the pub for murder and coining. (This particular offence involved scraping off of the outside of gold coins with a file and scissors). Busby has been seen wandering around the pub and village with a rope around his neck and his head low on his chest. He had been found guilty of murdering his father-in-law, Dan Auty, over some deal. The word 'stoop' is an old North Riding term for pole or post; so Busby Stoop means 'Busby's Gibbet'. Another story surrounds a chair at the pub that acquired an evil reputation in the early 1950s because the locals believed it had been influenced by the ghost of Busby. There was an accident to a local man about that time and later the chair was taken away to Thirsk museum on the orders of the then landlord, Tony Earnshaw, and placed where no one could sit there again.

Black Bull, Haworth

Drovers Inn, Dallowgill

An isolated inn out on the moors it provided food and shelter for cattle and sheep drovers over the centuries. There were several Iron Age settlements found nearby and bronze axes were found in the area in the late-nineteenth century. The last shop in Dallowgill was a farm selling sweets and cigarettes and that closed in the 1940s. Once there was a monument to mark the extinction of wolves in the area and this was replaced to commemorate Queen Victoria's Diamond Jubilee in 1897. The inn is haunted by someone arriving in the early hours of the morning, kicking on the door and shouting. Legend has it that a drover, who had got lost, found the inn and then wandered away. His body was later found a mile away in a snow drift.

Golden Fleece, York

Not far from the famous Shambles in York is the Golden Fleece, one of the city's oldest pubs. One of the first mentions of the Golden Fleece is in the York Archives of 1503. At one time the inn belonged to the Merchant Adventurers who were responsible for the highly important wool trade of the time, based on the river Ouse. Part of the inn is named after Lady Alice Peckett whose husband John was Lord Mayor of York and owned the inn about 1702. She has been seen wandering the inn along the corridors and staircases in the early hours of the morning. There are said to be five other ghosts haunting the building which is an old wooden-framed building without foundations.

King's Arms, Haworth

Built on three storeys of local millstone grit it is a typically dark-looking Yorkshire building from the seventeenth century. At one time there was a slaughterhouse at the rear of the inn and the cellars were used by undertakers when the village morgue was full. Previous landlords held *arvils*, or funeral feasts here. At the centerpiece of the food would have been a coffin-shaped currant cake with a black paper flag. There have been many tales of poltergeist activities and loud moaning coming from the cellars where the bodies had been stored.

Drovers Inn, Dallowgill

King's Arms, Haworth

Old Starre Inn, York

Old Silent Inn, Stanbury

Legend has it that when Bonnie Prince Charlie was escaping back to Scotland he stayed at this inn which was then called the Eagle. The local natives kept quiet about this and thus it adopted its present name. Over a century ago a landlady at the pub fed the wild cats and called them to her door by ringing a bell. Even today her ghostly clanging can be heard every now and again and it is attended by a noisy mustering of hungry feline ghosts. There have also been sighting of a large man with a travelling bag over his shoulder walking up the stairs of the inn. One pair of residents were awakened when their bedroom began to shake and a glass pot flew across the room to crash into the opposite wall. They went to the manager and together they all witnessed a painting moving about on the wall. At the same time the curtains began opening and closing of their own accord with no one nearby to move them.

Old Starre Inn, York

During the siege of York in the Civil War this pub was used as a hospital for the wounded. Medicine was, of course, still in its infancy and men had limbs chopped off while still conscious but perhaps helped with a bottle of rum. Occasionally their screams can be heard coming from the cellars below. There are also two phantom cats in the pub which have been pursued by some pub dogs, one of which knocked itself unconscious as he sprang against the wall. There is also an elderly woman in grey seen climbing the stairs.

Old White Lion, Haworth

Standing proud at the top of Haworth's world-famous cobbled street, the Old White Lion opened in the mid-1700s. By 1783 it was the White Lion Inn run by Jeremiah Jewett. Guests staying here have told waitresses, over breakfast, of strange happenings during the night. Usually they say they are just about to slip into sleep when they feel the dizzy sensation of falling through space and waking up. At this point they see a pretty, white-faced woman in Victorian clothing staring down at them. While staying here I overheard a conversation in the entrance hall from the residents' lounge. She said:

> Something queer and odd just happened. I was coming past room seven when this woman just appeared through the door from the inside. She just looked at me and then disappeared back through the door. I mean, it's an odd thing to happen at this time of day.

(Perhaps not so odd when you get people like Zerubbabel Barraclough buried in Haworth graveyard with other grave epitaphs such as 'The Wronged Maiden' and the 'Day he Died').

Turk's Head, Ripon

On the main road from Harrogate into Ripon this is an early-Victorian pub haunted by two urchins without footwear. They are thought to be two orphans who had been at the local workhouse or orphanage and hanged in the eighteenth century. Nearby is Barefoot Street leading to Gallows Hill and it is said that criminals had their boots or shoes taken from them here and walked barefoot to the hangman. The turk's head is also an ornate knot that looked like a turban worn by the Saracens. In the North of England such a pub is also nicknamed the 'Pasha's Napper'.

Wheatsheaf, Howden

Photographs of apparitions in the very act of haunting are rare but one has actually appeared in a picture of this village pub. It was built in the seventeenth century and stands near to the thousand-year-old Howden Minster. The shape of a ghost was photographed by a local journalist. The picture shows what appears to be part of the left shoulder and arm of a white-clad person leaving the bar. The licensees have heard footsteps in the pub in an upstairs corridor when no one has been about.

Top: *Turk's Head, Ripon*

Left: *Turk's Head, Ripon*

Above: *World's End, Knaresborough*

World's End, Knaresborough

Old Mother Shipton foretold that when Knaresborough Bridge collapses for the third time it will be end of the world. It has collapsed twice already so, hence the name of this pub. It is haunted by a woman who is seeking release from her earthly bondage. A medium went to the World's End by mistake thinking it was the the Mother Shipton pub in Knaresborough, and said that she sensed this ghost was seeking relief. Children who have stayed there have spoken to the wraith and one child would not stay in a room because of voices and lights. Landlord Eric Wilson has a grandfather clock which had been stopped and run down. Suddenly it started up again and was found to be fully wound. A woman walking through the house felt something brush across her face and when she got upstairs her mouth was bleeding. The story behind it is that in the fifteenth century a girl called Beatrice, who worked at the pub, became pregnant aged sixteen and hanged herself in the cellar.

York Arms, York

This inner-city pub, opposite the Minster, has the smallest bar in York and perhaps in the county. A grey lady haunts it and is said to be a nun who was walled up after she gave birth to a child in a former religious building on this site. Another story is that the nun had a vision of an angel, told her superiors then died of a broken heart when they would not believe her. It has been a priory and then a prison in its time. Items fly about the room of the pub and stools overturn as the ghost nun searches for her lost baby. One landlord, who saw the apparition, threw a paint brush at her and said she sneered as the brush went through her. It did, however, leave a paint smear on the wall.

LIST OF TAVERNS

Bedfordshire
Cross Keys, Pulloxhill

Berkshire
Bull, Wargrave
George Hotel, Wallingford
Leathern Bottle, Warfield
Seven Stars, Knowl Hill

Buckinghamshire
Chequers Inn, Amersham
George & Dragon, West Wycombe
Little Angel, Remenham
Ostrich, Colbrook
Royal Standard of England, Beaconsfield
Watts Arms, Hanslope

Cambridgeshire
Black Bull at Brampton and Dragoon, Brampton
Golden Lion Hotel, St Ives
Old Ferryboat, Holywell

Cheshire
Blue Bell Inn, Tushingham
Orange Tree, Altrincham
Royal George, Knutsford

Cornwall
Bucket of Blood, Phillack
Bush Inn, Morwenstow
Crumplehorn Inn, Polperro
Jamaica Inn, Bolventor
Jolly Sailor Inn, Looe
Miner's Arms, Mithian
Napoleon Inn, Boscastle
Punch Bowl Inn, Lanreath
Wellington Hotel, Boscastle

Cumbria
Dalston Hall, Dalston
Edenhall Hotel, Penrith
Gosforth Hall Hotel, Gosforth
Kirkstone Pass Inn, Ambleside
Moresby Hall, Moresby
Overwater Hall, Ireby

Derbyshire
Bell Hotel, Derby
Castle Inn, Castleton
Miner's Arms, Eyam
Norfolk Arms Hotel, Glossop

Devon
Bearslake Inn, Okehampton
Bridge Inn, Topsham
Church House Inn, Torbryan
Devil's Stone, Shebbear
Old Inn, Widecombe in the Moor
Pack o' Cards, Combe Martin
Prospect Inn, Exeter
Royal Castle Hotel, Dartmouth

Ship Inn, Exeter
White Hart Hotel, Exeter
Who'd Have Thought It, Milton Combe

Dorset
Angel Inn, Lyme Regis
Ye Olde George Inn, Christchurch.

Durham
George Hotel, Piercebridge

Essex
Bell Hotel, Thorpe-le-Soken
St Anne's Castle Inn, Great Leighs
Sun Hotel, Dedham
Swan Hotel, Brentwood

Gloucestershire
Berkeley Arms, Tewkesbury
Butcher's Arms, Painswick
King's Arms Hotel, Stow-on-the-Wold
Corner Cupboard Inn, Winchcombe
Royalist, Stow-on-the-Wold
Tudor House Hotel, Tewkesbury
Ye Olde Black Bear, Tewkesbury

Hampshire
Angel, Lymington
Brushmaker's Arms, Upham
Crown Hotel, Alton
Dolphin, Botley
Dolphin Hotel, Southampton
Eclipse Inn, Winchester
Filly Inn, Setley
Fleurs De Lys, Pilley
Hyde Tavern, Winchester
Old Mill Inn, Holbury
Queen's Head, Burley
Red Lion, Chalton
Royal Anchor Hotel, Liphook
Royal Oak, Langstone
Tudor Rose, Fordingbridge
Waggon and Horses, Walhampton
White Hart Hotel, Andover

Hertfordshire
Brocket Arms, Ayot St Lawrence
Chequers Inn, Anstey
Hollybush Inn, Elstree
White Lion, Walkern

Isle of Wight
Hare and Hounds, Downend

Kent
Bell Inn, Hythe
Bishop's Finger, Canterbury
Black Horse, Pluckley
Captain Digby, Kingsgate
Chequers, Doddington
Chequers, Sevenoaks
Cooper's Arms, Rochester
Cricketers Inn, Meopham
Crown Inn, Shoreham
Dering Arms, Pluckley
George Hotel, Margate
King's Head, Grafty Green
Kings Head, Hythe
Northern Belle, Margate
Pied Bull, Farningham
Red Lion, Lenham
Red Lion, Rusthall
Shipwright's Arms, Oare
Three Cruches, Strood
Walnut Tree, Aldington
White Hart, Newenden
White Horse, Chilham
White Horse, Dover
Woolpack, Chilham
Ye Olde Chequers, Tonbridge

Lancashire
Q, Stalybridge
Star & Garter, Stockport
Thatched House, Stockport

Leicestershire
White Hart, Ashby de la Zouche

Lincolnshire
Abbey Hotel, Crowland
Angel & Royal, Grantham
Black Horse Grimsthorpe
Sun, Saxby
White Hart Hotel, Lincoln

London
Anchor Inn SE1
Anchor Tap, Bermondsey
Angel, Bermondsey Wall, East SE16
Angel WC2

Black Lion W6
Bow Bells E3
Flask, Highgate N6
Gatehouse, Highgate Hill N6
George Inn, Southwark SE1
Globe Inn, Southwark SE1
Golden Lion, King Street SW1
Grenadier SW1
Hand & Shears, Middle Street EC1
Lamb Tavern EC3
Market Porter, Stoney Street SE1
Old Nun's Head, Nunhead Green
Old Queen's Head, Canonbury N1
Opera Tavern WC2
Tabard, Chiswick W4
Volunteer NW1
Warrington Hotel W9
White Hart E1
William 4th NW3
Ye Olde Cock Tavern EC4

Middlesex
Bell Inn, Hounslow

Norfolk
Duke's Head, Kings Lynn
Goat Inn, Brundall
Hall Inn, Sea Palling
King's Head, Hethersett
Scole Inn, Scole
Victoria, Happisburgh

Northamptonshire
Bell at Finedon, Finedon,
Black Lion Inn, Northampton
Ship Hotel, Oundle,
Talbot, Oundle

Northumberland
Ye Olde Cross, Alnwick

Nottinghamshire
Nag's Head, Nottingham
Ye Olde Ramme, Mansfield
Ye Old Salutation, Nottingham
Ye Olde Trip to Jerusalem, Nottingham

Oxfordshire
Barley Mow, Clifton, Hampden
Bird Cage, Thame

Bull, Henley on Thames
George Hotel, Dorchester on Thames
Hopcrofts Holt, Steeple Aston
King's Arms, Oxford
Old Crown Coaching Inn, Faringdon
Plough, Upper Wolvercote
Tite Inn, Chadlington
Weston Manor Hotel, Weston on the Green
White Hart, Minster Lovell

Shropshire
Feathers Hotel, Ludlow

Somerset
Bird in Hand, Glastonbury
Castle Hotel, Castle Green
Chough Hotel, Chard
George & Pilgrim, Glastonbury
George Inn, Wedmore
Holman Clavell Inn, Blagdon Hill

Staffordshire
Royal Oak Inn, Abbots Bromley
Whittington Inn, Kinver

Suffolk
Angel Inn, Lavenham
Bell Inn, Walberswick
Bull, Long Melford
Crown Hotel, Bildeston
Nutshell, Bury St Edmunds
White Hart, Blythburgh
Ye Olde Three Tuns, Bungay

Surrey
Angel Inn, Guildford
Barley Mow, Englefield Green
Bell Inn, East Molesey
Britannia, Richmond
Crown Inn, Old Oxted
George Inn, Chertsey
Greyhound Inn, Carshalton
Greyhound Inn, Lingfield

King's Arms Royal Hotel, Godalming
King's Head, Chertsey
Marquis of Granby, Esher
Queen's Head, Weybridge
Roebuck, Richmond
White Hart, Wood Street

Sussex

Angel, Petworth
Bat & Ball, Brighton
Bath Arms, Brighton
Bell Inn, Iden
Blackboys, Blackboys
Black Lion, Brighton
Blue Anchor, Portslade
Bow Street Runner, Hove
Brunswick, Hove
Bull Hotel, Ditchling
Cat Inn, West Hoathly
Cock Inn, Wivelsfield Green
Colonnade Bar, Brighton
Cricketers, Brighton
Crown & Anchor, Shoreham
Dr Brightons, Brighton
Druid's Head, Brighton
Dyke Tavern, Brighton
George & Dragon, Dragon's Green
Golden Cannon, Brighton
Golden Lion, Brighton
Greyhound, Brighton
Hangleton Manor, Hove
Horse and Groom, Brighton
John's Cross Inn, John's Cross, Near Robertsbridge
Lion, Brighton
Marlborough, Brighton
Mermaid Inn, Rye
New Inn, Hurstpierpoint
Old Ship, Brighton
Plough Inn, Pycombe
Queen's Head, Icklesham
Ram Inn, West Firle
Regency Tavern, Brighton
Royal Oak, East Lavant
Royal Oak, Poynings
Royal Oak, Wivelsfield
Schooner, Shoreham

Seven Stars, Robertsbridge
Shades, Crawley
Shelley's Bar, Lewes
Shepherd & Dog, Fulking
Six Bells, Chiddingley
Spread Eagle, Midhurst
Stag, Hastings
Stag's Head, Portslade
Star, Alfriston
Union Inn, Rye
War-Bill-in-Tun, Warbleton
White Hart, Lewes
White Horse, Ditchling
Ye Castle, Bramber

Warwickshire

Castle Inn, Edgehill
Sheaf and Sickle, Long Lawford

Wiltshire

Haunch of Venison, Salisbury
King & Queen, Highworth
Red Lion, Avebury

Yorkshire

Black Bull, Haworth
Black Swan, Peaseholme Green
Busby Stoop, Carlton Miniott
Drovers Inn, Dallowgill
Golden Fleece, York
King's Arms, Haworth
Old Silent Inn, Stanbury
Old Starre Inn, York
Old White Lion, Haworth
Turk's Head, Ripon
Wheatsheaf, Howden
World's End, Knaresborough
York Arms, York

If you are interested in purchasing other books published by Tempus, or in case you have difficulty finding any Tempus books in your local bookshop, you can also place orders directly through our website

www.tempus-publishing.com